ARUNDEL'S GREAT WAR

FORWARD

Arundel's World War One record is a proud one, in all out of a population of 2665 no less than 695 men either volunteered or were already serving as part of the regular forces when war was declared, with not one man having to be conscripted.

During the four years conflict Arundel's soldiers and sailors were awarded with 12 Military Crosses, 5 Military Medals, 6 DCMs and 4 Military Crosses. The War Memorial standing proudly in the Square records the names of the men who paid the supreme sacrifice. This book, based on the Arundel War Memorials, tells their stories in real time; it also reproduces their letters home and newspaper articles about individuals and includes some other men who had obvious Arundel connections, who were discovered during the researching.

Neither have the wives and families left at home been forgotten, with a year by year summary of home events.

This book has taken a considerable amount time to complete and every care has been taken to ensure its accuracy.

Those men who enlisted from Tortington have been excluded; their war service being told in an excellent book 'Tortington in the Great War 1914-1918' which has recently been written by local resident John Henderson and I certainly recommend it.

Unless otherwise stated, all quotes come from the *West Sussex Gazette*.

Cliff Mewett
2017

PART ONE

DECLARATION, MOBILISATION & RECRUITMENT

During the last few days of July 1914 life in Arundel was continuing as normal. The Arundel St Philip's Cricket Club had registered an emphatic win against Poling and Lyminster, posting a target of 155 runs and bowling their opponents out for just 46! New troop flags were presented to the Earl of Arundel's Own Troop of Boy Scouts in an impressive parade at the Castle and great excitement occurred when a horse drawing one of Arundel Corporation's water carts ran away down King Street, before crashing into a wall in Maltravers Street.

ARUNDEL POST OFFICE WHICH STAYED OPEN NEARLY ALL NIGHT AWAITING NEWS OF THE DECLARATION OF WAR

Meanwhile, across the Channel war fever was mounting, as the opposing European nations assumed their respective entrenched positions. Great Britain had stood a little apart from events in Europe, but the King's decision not to attend Goodwood Week because of the foreign crisis and the call-up of Naval Reservists in a Test Mobilisation, did not go unnoticed in Arundel and as July turned into August war seemed a certainty.

Germany violated neutral Belgium's territory on 4 August in an attempt to invade France, thereby triggering a longstanding treaty that Great Britain had to guarantee Belgium's sovereignty. In response to this the British Government issued an ultimatum demanding Germany should withdraw or a state of war would exist between them; the whole Country was awaiting the German response which reached Arundel by an official telegram:

'Large numbers of people waited outside the Post Office which was open all night for the result of the British ultimatum. It was not until 3am that the message which had been despatched from London at 11 30pm arrived, stating England's Declaration of War'.

THE 5TH LONDON INFANTRY BRIGADE AT ARUNDEL 1913

The annual camps of various Territorial Regiments had taken place at Arundel for many years. In 1914 the 6th (Cyclist) Battalion, the Royal Sussex Regiment, comprising some two hundred Officers and men had arrived in Arundel Park on 11 July, complete with ordinary bicycles, four motor bicycles and two machine guns, included with their general equipment. Their time was spent carrying out various manoeuvres and concluded with their annual sports day.

The 4th Battalion, the Royal Sussex Regiment, were formed on 1 April 1908 and were part of the Territorial Force, 'F' Company being centred on Arundel and included some men from Storrington. They signed on for four years and paraded weekly at the Drill Hall in London Road, under Captain GS Constable and Lieutenant EH Mostyn and also attended an annual summer camp. They had left town that same week to join the Home Counties Division at Bordon, Hampshire, where they were due to stay until 2 August. From there they were planned to transfer to Salisbury for another seven days, where an estimated 50,000 Officers and men were to be assembled. However, with the Declaration of War they were recalled early as part of the national mobilisation, arriving back in Arundel two days later.

'F' COMPANY (ARUNDEL) 4ᵀᴴ BATTALION, THE ROYAL SUSSEX REGIMENT

'Enthusiasm reigned in the town on Tuesday evening 6 August when it was learned that the local F Company, 4th Battalion, the Royal Sussex Regiment, the Territorial's, were returning from their annual camp and were to be billeted in the Town Hall for the night. A crowd of interested people waited up to welcome them when they returned well after midnight having been on the move for twenty four hours with little food. They evoked the admiration of proud relatives and everyone else by their vigour and alertness as, to the tune of a gaily whistled march they came through the town and took possession of their temporary barracks.

The following afternoon the Company marched to Ford Station, where they entrained for Newhaven. There was an impressive scene outside the Town Hall, where a large assembly of relatives and friends gave them a good send off. On all sides there was a conspicuous absence of gloominess, everyone appearing to be in good spirits, celebrating the arrival of war with great delight. Many patriots of the town made their premises gay with flags'

This scene was enacted throughout the Country;

'The mobilisation of the Territorial Force is now on the point of

completion with. every unit believed to be up to establishment. As is known, certain units of the Territorial Force have for some time accepted a liability to serve overseas if required and further volunteers are now being asked to follow their example. A great response is anticipated and it is probable that in many cases, Brigades and even Divisions as a whole will come forward'. PRESS BUREAU.

The Arundel Company were led to war by the Town Mayor, Captain Guy Constable, whose family owned the local Swallow Brewery. By going to war he relinquished his position as Mayor, the serving Deputy Mayor, Mr WW Mitchell, the senior proprietor of the *West Sussex Gazette*, stepping up for the remainder of the year. At the following Council meeting the new Mayor moved:

'That the Council regrets the absence of the Mayor, but is proud to know he is on active service at the head of the Arundel Company of his Regiment and wishes him and all Arundel men now serving in their Country's defence a safe return. He has led his native town in peace and has linked it to the service of the State in the nation's need, for he commands a Company most closely identified with the town'.

**5 AUGUST 1914 - F COMPANY (ARUNDEL) 4TH BATTALION
ROYAL SUSSEX REGIMENT PREPARE TO MARCH TO WAR**

The Territorial's were initially based at Newhaven, an important port and a prime target for an enemy invasion force. 'F' Company were amalgamated with Chichester to become 'D' Company, 4th Battalion, the Royal Sussex Regiment and re-located to Cambridge, where they undertook training and were also used to boost recruitment.

The men of the Sussex Yeomanry and the Royal Army Service Corps arrived in town the following day and requisitioned about forty horses in the neighbourhood. After a horse had been certified by a veterinary surgeon a price was fixed and whether the owner was satisfied or not he had to part with the animal. All the horses were then entrained to Canterbury, Kent, in readiness for war duty.

Other soldiers also arrived in town in the form of members of 9th Hampshire Territorials, (Cyclists), some fifty eight members in all, as part of the home defence. They were billeted locally, with the Norfolk Hotel supplying their meals.

=====

With the departure of the Territorial's, Arundel began to organise itself on a war footing. A Recruiting Office was set up in the High Street under the watchful eye of retired Naval Warrant Officer, Richard Wilson, who also ran a general shop at 15 Gatwick Terrace, South Marshes. Initially, recruitment had been a little slow, but as soon as the harvest had been gathered in the pace quickened and volunteers left in small groups every few days. They were always given a patriotic send off by families, townsfolk and the school children, who gathered in the Square to cheer them on their way.

'Fourteen recruits were sent off from Arundel on Monday amid much popular enthusiasm. Members of the 1st and 2nd Arundel Troops of Boy Scouts, with their bands, preceded the recruits to Arundel Railway Station. Before the recruits went off the Mayor made a few remarks and the Mayoress shook each recruit by the hand and gave him her good wishes'.

The Officers and men of the 3rd Home Service Battalion, the Royal Sussex Regiment, took part in a week long Recruitment March, visiting the towns and villages of West Sussex, gathering recruits. After an overnight stay at Worthing, they marched to Littlehampton and rested, before moving on to Arundel, where a recruitment meeting and overnight stay were planned.

'The lads fell in punctually and to the stirring note of bugle and drum they started for the town of Arundel. Crowds lined the route whilst many a window fluttered the old flag. Not a few among the crowd were school children, who had obtained leave to see brother go by. At Arundel their welcome was, if anything, even heartier and the streets of the town blossomed to welcome the two hundred and twenty Officers and men; house after house displayed a string of flags along the front garden wall, whilst from such places as the Brewery there was, flying in the breeze, bunting of quite imposing proportions. They marched in over the Arundel Bridge at about four o'clock, to the sound of drums and bugles, a smart soldierly looking Company and were greeted by a large gathering in the Square'.

Favoured with fine weather, several hundred people attended the evening meeting in the Market Square.

THE ARUNDEL SCOUTS AND THEIR BAND WHICH ACCOMPANIED RECRUITS TO THE RAILWAY STATION

'A farm wagon, with a green canopy and a backcloth, was the stand for the speakers, the Duke of Norfolk presiding. Urgent appeals were made for recruits. The Duke, who addressed the gathering as "Friends All" said that the question to all of them, was as important and anxious as any ever discussed in Arundel, in Sussex, or in England. On that question depended the whole life and liberty of the Country'

The special object of the meeting was to urge those men whose time of life would allow them, to come forward and take up arms in defence of their Country. The Duke was not speaking in any tone of complaint. On the contrary, he was proud to know that Arundel had shown a very fine spirit and he expressed his sincere gratitude for the great number of men working for him who had gone away to serve their Country. He thanked them very heartily and was proud of them and asked all employers of labour who were unable to bear arms themselves to give encouragement and facilities to their employees who were able to do so.

Mr A M Paddon followed the Duke of Norfolk with an eloquent and hard hitting speech, concluding;

'It is England's duty to show what her voluntary system could do against the coercion of other races; it's the day of the soldier',

Captain HE Mathews, in command of the Battalion, followed with a few soldierly words.

'We want men for home service, so as to free the Battalion at Newhaven for Foreign Service. That Battalion are thirsting to get abroad, but they

could not go until the Reserve Battalion was at full strength. They had five hundred men, but wanted five hundred more and I am confident they will get them and I would ask wives to use a little inducement to encourage their husbands'.

The meeting ended and the crowd moved down to the Recruiting Office, where sixteen men were immediately enrolled.

The following morning when the men were drawn up on the Square in the bright sunshine before leaving for Chichester, the Duke of Norfolk addressed a few words to them. They were then presented with gifts of tobacco from his Grace and chocolate from the Mayor. The soldiers raised three hearty cheers, after which they marched through Tarrant Street towards Chichester.

The sixteen recruits left Arundel two days later, played to the station by the Scouts Band, a scenario to be repeated weekly for the next few months as groups of a dozen or more, usually seen off by the Mayor and the Recruiting Officer left for the war, including the three Arundel policemen, PC's Holdstock, Jones and Peters, who volunteered and enlisted into the Grenadier Guards.

Among the other men who enlisted early, apart from members of the Dukes Estate staff, included ten postmen from Arundel Post Office and thirty members of the West Sussex Gazette, which published;

'How many other provincial towns can show a finer record, or have set a more commendable example in ready patriotism to the nation at large? And what community, in this or any other Country, has gone about the work of mobilising its fighting forces with less fuss?'

1914 WAR FRONT

Meanwhile the members of the British Expeditionary Force (BEF) started arriving in France on 9 August and by the 22 August some 160,000 men had been ferried across the Channel, closely chaperoned by the powerful Royal Navy. Compared to the large conscripted armies of the other countries the BEF was small in numbers, described by the Kaiser as 'a contemptible little army'. They were soon in action during the German advance, which had been rapid in pursuance of the aims of their Schlieffen Plan, being the swift defeat of France in the west, before turning their attentions to the Russian forces in the east.

The British Expeditionary Force's first major engagement with the enemy was at Mons, where they attempted to hold the line of the Mons-Conde Canal. Despite being outnumbered they inflicted heavy casualties on the Germans before being forced to retreat. They set up defensive positions at Le Cateau, but were heavily attacked on 26 August and had to withdraw westwards. Having retreated continuously for ten to twelve days and under repeated German attack, the BEF were on the point of exhaustion when they reached the River Marne. The Germans were now only thirty miles east of Paris and the French Government, expecting the capital to fall, left for Bordeaux. On 4 September the French launched a counter attack and in turning to meet it the Germans opened up a thirty mile wide gap between their First and Second Armies. Quick to exploit this, the BEF poured through between the two German armies and boosted by some 6000 French Infantry Reservists, who arrived from Paris in a fleet of 600 taxi-cabs, the German advance was halted. By 9 September they began to retreat towards the River Aisne. This was a significant Allied victory and ended any German hopes of a swift victory on the Western Front. However, casualties were high in the BEF with 12,773 men losing their lives.

The First Battle of Ypres was the last of a series of battles between the Allies and Germans in the Race to the Sea. Both sides wanted the Channel Ports, the British in particular needing them as they were the main supply lines from the United Kingdom. The Belgian town of Ypres was the last obstacle in the Germans' way. Fighting began in earnest on 19 October, when the Germans launched their first attack on the Allied lines. Over the next month further attacks and counter-attacks took place, the fighting petering out as winter weather began to take effect. Trench fighting would soon take over.

======

The first Arundel fatality occurred on 21 October 1914, 'news had been received of the death of Sapper Harry MILLS', who was the eldest son of brewer's clerk, Harry (senior) and his wife Emma, the family living in Maltravers Street. On leaving school, Harry became a butcher's boy, but by 1911 was serving as a carpenter in the Royal Engineers, based at Colchester, as part of the Eastern Command. When war broke out, the 9th Field Company were attached to the British 4th Division, which had assembled in France by 22 August and were quickly sent to the Front. The Division fought at the Battle of Le Cateau where it lost some 3000 men. From there they moved to the area of the Aisne and then to Ypres, where Sapper Harry Mills was killed in action, aged 29.

======

Guardsman Percy AYLWARD was born in Arundel, the son of Mr and Mrs Richard Aylward and although his parents moved to Chichester during his childhood, Percy enlisted at Arundel into the Scots Guards sometime before 1911.

When war was declared his Regiment were stationed at Aldershot and were swiftly mobilised arriving at Le Havre on 14 August. They moved to the Front and fought at Mons and Ypres, where they stubbornly resisted the German advance. It was in this action on 11 November 1914 that Guardsman Percy AYLWARD aged 28, became the second Arundel man to lose his life.

=====

The name Frank NORTHEAST appears on both the Arundel War Memorial and the Cathedral War Memorials; he possibly lived at 25 Bond Street. He was the son of Richard and Emma and was 26 years old when he lost his life in 1914.

=====

Meanwhile the war at sea was also taking its toll of local men.

HMS Good Hope, a Drake Class heavy cruiser, was laid down in September 1899 and launched in February 1901, spending many years in the Atlantic Squadron before being placed in reserve in 1913. She was re-commissioned during the Test Mobilisation just before the outbreak of hostilities and left Portsmouth on 2 August on her way to join the 6th Cruiser Squadron at Scapa Flow, as part of the Grand Fleet. However, she was almost immediately detached from the main fleet and sent to reinforce the South American Squadron under Rear Admiral Sir Christopher Cradock, becoming his flagship. At that time it was thought that German liners leaving the eastern ports of the United States could easily convert themselves into armed merchant cruisers, installing guns stowed away in their holds and therefore needed to be dealt with. The job of HMS Good Hope for the first few weeks of the war was to protect British merchant shipping as far south as the Falkland Islands, where she and the rest of the Squadron docked at Port Stanley.

For some months the Royal Navy had been searching for the German East Asiatic Squadron under Admiral von Spee, which had been operating in the Pacific. Information had now been received that the Germans were planning to sail into the South Atlantic to prey upon shipping in the British trading routes along the east coast of South America. The Royal Navy South American Squadron consisted of the cruiser HMS Monmouth, the light cruiser HMS Glasgow, a converted ex-liner the Otranto, boosted by the newly arrived HMS Good Hope. These ships were no match for the modern German Squadron, which contained five up-to-date cruisers, including the Scharnhorst and Gneisenau, which could each concentrate six 8.2 inch guns on a single target at once.

Rear Admiral Cradock waited at Port Stanley in the hope of naval reinforcements, but despite his lack of firepower was ordered to seek and attack the German Squadron. On 18 October the British Squadron left Port Stanley to rendezvous with HMS Glasgow, which had been sent on patrol earlier to gather intelligence. The British made contact with the Germans at the Coronel, off the Chilean coast, just before sunset on 1 November and chose to stay and fight in the failing light, after ordering the Otranto to break formation and flee. In difficult seas the engagement began. Using their greater firepower and staying just out of reach of the British guns, HMS Good Hope was crippled by the Scharnhorst's third salvo and blazing from stem to stern in the failing light, exploded and sank with all 900 hands.

======

Among the crew of HMS Good Hope was First Class Petty Officer James Frederick BERRYMAN, the son of Mr and Mrs John Berryman, of Park Place, Arundel. His father, at one time, was a brewer's drayman and his mother died whilst he was a child. James was the husband of Edith and they lived close to the Naval Base at 5 Agincourt Road, Portsmouth. Like many of the crew of HMS Good Hope, 34 year old James was a member of the Royal Naval Volunteer Reserve and recalled to service at the outbreak of war.

======

HMS Monmouth was built in 1901 and launched in 1903. She was the head ship in a new class of ten armoured cruisers and spent the next seven years in the Far East, based at the China Station. On returning home she was also placed in reserve and was then re-commissioned at the outbreak of war, being assigned to Admiral Cradock's flotilla. Like HMS Good Hope she was crewed by many reservists as well as regular sailors; they fought a gallant action. Early on she received a direct hit on her main forward turret from the Gneisenau which blew off her roof and started a fire, causing an ammunition explosion. Her crew extinguished the fire but the ship was listing in heavy seas, thus making her port side guns inoperable. Having witnessed the loss of HMS Good Hope the Monmouth fought on and was approached by the Nurnberg who tried to get her to surrender. HMS Monmouth turned and avoiding a torpedo increased speed to attack the Nurnberg, but she was hit by gunfire and still listing badly, overturned and went down with her flag flying. The seas were too rough for any rescue attempt and her crew of 758 lost their lives. The Battle of Coronel had cost the lives of over 1600 sailors in a couple of hours.

======

On board HMS Monmouth was Musician Alfred George CARVER of the Royal Marines, the son of gas engine driver Alfred and Elizabeth, of 17 Ford Road. Alfred, who had an older brother and sister, spent some of his childhood living at California Terrace. He had joined the Royal Navy as a boy sailor, based at the Royal Marine Artillery Barracks at Eastney, Portsmouth, where he studied music, becoming a member of the Royal Marine Band. His cause of death was listed as 'killed or died as a direct result of enemy action, his body was not recovered for burial'.
A former member of the Parish Church choir, a Memorial Service was held there for him on 8 December 1914.

====

1914 HOME FRONT

The summer visitors, so important to the town's economy, had continued to arrive over the August Bank Holiday, despite the threat of imminent war.

'Our holiday visitors were fully up to the average in numbers and were favoured with weather, which, though uncertain, favoured sunshine more than shower. Park and river and woods were sought. It was a quieter holiday crowd than usual, for the shadow of the immeasurable European calamity was upon it'.

With the Declaration of War most made their way home.

It was not only the volunteers who left town, but equipment as well, notably the most powerful of GS Constable and Sons conveyances, a Foden steam wagon, which was requisitioned by the War Office for military purposes and left Arundel on 4 October 1914.

With so many Arundel men now with the Colours, home security was high on the agenda. The newly formed West Sussex Volunteer Civil Guard extended to Arundel, where Colonel GH Turner of the Indian Army (retired) expressed an interest and his willingness to command, with Sgt T S Smith, who lived at 75 Maltravers Street, as his National Reserve Instructor. This was specifically aimed at men of non military service age, who were prepared to train as a Home Defence Unit. Consequently a Town Guard was formed;

'Arundel has taken steps for town protection at a well attended meeting held at the Town Hall, where a resolution was passed to the effect that a Town Protection Committee be formed to give such aid as national and local bodies may call for and to undertake such duties as may properly fall to all who are not serving their Country in other ways'.

The meeting formed the following sub committees, recruiting, fire protection, Red Cross work and rifle shooting and by the end of 1914 had enrolled thirty members.

The Arundel Miniature Rifle Club swung into action and with thanks to the Duke of Norfolk were given the use of the range situated in Arundel Park. This was normally used by the local Territorial's and those units who held annual camps in the Arundel district, now the Town Guard were given access, but only after they had qualified on their miniature range. In order to get the scheme underway, three residents lent rifles for training purposes, the ammunition and financial needs being left to the relevant subcommittee to arrange, the members firing approximately 1500 rounds per week!

'Every lad of fifteen and every man who is left in Arundel has the opportunity now to learn how to shoot and surely that is his duty'.

Within a week or so forty residents had answered the call.

During the early months of the war the shops of Arundel were reported to be doing brisk business, particularly with food orders, a short lived period of panic buying became evident;

'Here, as elsewhere, some selfish unpatriotic people rushed to give

excessive orders for food supplies. We hear that one local firm, when abnormal demands were made, refused to supply more than one half or one quarter of the goods ordered. Any panic has now passed and prices are reverting to normal, one firm only raising its prices where it was absolutely obliged'.

This panic soon settled down as people realised that there would not be an immediate food shortage. However, as Christmas approached the Arundel bakers issued this notice;

'We, the undersigned, bakers and confectioners of Arundel, very much regret to announce that, owing to the high cost of raw materials and other expenses, we agree to discontinue Christmas Boxes this year.

A Dumbrell, Tarrant Street, EJ Greenfield, High Street, Gray and Company, High Street and DP Osbourne, King Street'

Voluntary activity by the townsfolk in response to the declaration began immediately in anticipation of casualties arriving in Arundel;

'The Arundel Red Cross Society, whose Quartermaster, Mrs Guy Constable, has made an urgent appeal for blankets, sheets, pillowcases, towels, nightshirts, socks, dusters and money have set up two collection points, one in Arundel and the other at St John's Priory, Poling. These are not required now, but are to be registered and will be requisitioned at twenty four hours notice in the case of a local emergency. It is important that the response should be speedy'.

All items throughout the war were sent on to Chichester, where a main depot was established.

One Red Cross member, Mr T Pierce was detached for service at the Netley War Hospital, Southampton. However, it wasn't long before Arundel prepared for its own medical centre:

An Arundel hospital was also established at the girl's club room at St Wilfred's Convent;

'Hospital beds have been provided at the Convent for twelve wounded soldiers. The Duchess of Norfolk is generously supporting this little hospital in the way of food and surgical dressings, but the co-operation of the residents of Arundel and District would be welcomed. They will speedily find that there are many ways of rendering assistance. The Duchess is also providing three trained nurses, but additional help will be required from the members of the Red Cross Detachment. Mrs Pearson, the wife of Doctor Pearson will be the Lady Superintendant'.

However, the first 'casualties' of war to arrive in Arundel were not soldiers but Belgian refugees fleeing from the German invasion of their country;

'A family of Belgian refugees, father, mother and five children are now installed in a house in Surrey Street. They are Flemish speaking people from Malines, named Lauwers. Three more refugees, relatives of those already here, are coming to Arundel, where another house in Surrey Street has been provided for their reception. Many generous gifts have been

made by local people'.

Further refugees arrived with accommodation being arranged at the Trinity Chapel Manse. Financial support was offered from local businesses as well as weekly contributions from townsfolk, towards items such as furniture and crockery. The residents of Burpham raised £18 towards the refugees by staging a concert in their School Room;

'A skilfully varied programme was rendered by a number of ladies and gentlemen whose united efforts produced an evening's entertainment of a quality seldom obtained at village concerts of the kind. A note of seriousness dwelt upon by the Vicar of Burpham, the Reverend Clifford Toogood, who occupied the interval with a commendably brief yet very moving and eloquent address on the condition of affairs in Belgium and the events which had brought such complete and unmerited disaster on our heroic ally'.

The newly formed Arundel Distress Committee also decided to help provide for more refugees, their intentions being stopped, at least temporarily, by a Home Office statement which advised against accommodating further Belgium refugees on the South and East Coasts.

Other foreigners were not so welcome; the police in the Arundel Division arrested four aliens, three Germans and an Austrian, taking them into custody for the duration.

Another voluntary organisation was the Arundel War Depot, consisting of ladies who spent their time knitting mufflers and mittens for the men at the Front, under the direct control of the War Office. They were based in Mrs Carter's refreshment rooms in Mill Lane, meeting regularly several times a week. Any lady was welcome to join; all they had to do was turn up, equipped with 'suitable knitting needles'.

So successful was the Depot that the War Office gave them a large order for mufflers and mittens, to be executed 'in as short a time as possible'.

The pressure to recruit every man possible was further applied in November when two hundred Officers, NCO's and men of the 4th Battalion, the Royal Sussex Regiment, including Arundel Territorials, visited for an overnight recruiting drive which took place in the Market Square evening, once again presided by the Duke of Norfolk;

'Arundel still has an appreciable number of men fit and eligible to bear arms and an appeal is to be made to their patriotism'

But as 1914 drew to a close Arundel was noticeably short of men, reflecting the patriotic attitude of the population to date, with some three hundred now in uniform. A list, updated regularly, of those serving in His Majesty's Forces was posted in the Town Square.

Several men had been wounded and were in various hospitals, the Deputy Mayor initiating a fund to supply them with comforts. The West Sussex Gazette published an article 'The Toll of War' in which it listed the names of nine local men who had been wounded, one who was missing and the six who had lost their lives. The reality of war was settling over the town

1915 WAR FRONT

The 2nd Battalion, the Royal Sussex Regiment were stationed at Woking, when war broke out. Amid the rumours of war in the weeks preceding the declaration the Battalion had made ready, with stores, horses and transport arranged.

By 10 August 1914 the Battalion was ready for service and marched out of Inkerman Barracks becoming part of the British Army 1st Division. They travelled by train to Southampton and thence to Le Havre aboard the SS Olympia and SS Agapenor.

The Battalion fought at Marne, Aisne and Ypres in 1914, with further operations during the winter and into 1915 where they saw action at Aubers and Loos.

======

Serving with the 2nd Royal Sussex was Lance Corporal Arthur James HAYES the son of solicitors clerk James and his wife Annie. The family lived at Wellington Road, Hounslow, where Arthur was born in 1896. They then moved to Bognor where Annie ran a boarding house at 69 London Road, whilst James worked as a surveyor.

Arthur enlisted in Bognor, his connection with Arundel has not been established, although his name appears on the Arundel War Memorial. He was in action throughout January and the Battalion were instrumental in beating off a determined German attack on a Keep they were defending. They then spent a few weeks in reserve and training in February whilst receiving some reinforcements. Lance Corporal Hayes appears to have been killed 12 February 1915 in one of the several actions that occurred.

======

Born in Arundel, Private George SCUTT, was the son of Alfred, a newsagent; the family living variously in King Street, Maltravers Street and later the Slip Yard. On leaving school George became a butcher's assistant as well as joining the 4th Battalion, the Royal Sussex Regiment. He married his wife, Ethel and they had a son who was just four years old when George went off to war. George became ill and died on 29 March 1915, at Steyning, aged 28, before the Battalion went abroad, his cause of death is unknown

======

The north Kent town of Sheerness witnessed several ship tragedies during its links with the Royal Navy, the loss of HMS Princess Irene being one of them.

A new ship, originally built for the Canadian Pacific Railway, she was requisitioned by the Royal Navy on completion in 1914 and converted into a mine layer. At around 11 15am on **27 May 1915** she was anchored off Sheerness with almost her complete complimtent of 225 men, plus some 80 visiting Petty Officers and nearly that number of dockyard workers completing the conversion aboard. At that time new mines were being primed prior to her sailing a day or two later. There then occurred an almighty explosion, witnesses say the flames rose nearly two miles high. Parts of bodies were scattered over a wide area, there being just one survivor. The cause of the explosion was stated to be a faulty primer, although the work of priming the mines was being performed hastily by untrained men. The ship still lays submerged off Sheerness.

=====

Petty Officer Sail Makers Mate Sydney Montague Hardwick HILL, aged 33, was killed in this incident. He was the son of a retired Major, who was subsequently 'managing a public company' and his wife, Ellen. Sydney was born in Highgate, London, the family moving to Broadwater, Worthing by 1891. On leaving school Sydney enlisted into the Royal Navy and was serving as an Ordinary Seaman in 1901, his ship operating around Aden. It is not known whether he was serving on the Princess Irene or was one of the eighty visiting Petty Officers.

=====

Gallipoli was a disaster; Turkey, Germany's ally, had attacked Russia and was thrown back with a large loss of life. Russia appealed for assistance and a British landing with Australian, New Zealand and French support in the Gallipoli Peninsula was launched. Had it been successful, Egypt, which had already been subject to a Turkish attempt to seize the Suez Canal, would be safe and Russia would have had a warm water seaway to export much needed wheat to the Allies and in turn to receive arms and ammunition. The Campaign commenced with British naval actions in February 1915 and ended in a complete withdrawal of Allied forces in January 1916. It was particularly devastating in terms of losses relating to troops from Australia and New Zealand, the 25 April, Anzac Day, still commemorated in those countries.

=====

There were many men, who, having left these shores for a new life abroad, felt the need to return and fight for the mother country. One such man was Private Richard James Reginald READ who served with the 7th Australian Infantry, ANZAC Army Corps.

Born in Arundel, Richard grew up living in the High Street, where his father was a master butcher, Richard becoming a butcher's assistant on leaving school. However, the wider world called him and by 1909 he had emigrated to Australia, living in Northcote, Victoria, where he married his wife, Elsie, shortly before enlisting in the Australian Forces.

The combined Australian and New Zealand troops sailed for England on 10 November 1914 in ten transport ships accompanied by Australian,

Japanese and British warships. Concerns that the German cruiser SMS Emden was loose in the area were allayed after she was sunk by the Australian cruiser HMAS Sydney. The Anzacs as they became known got as far as Egypt when it was decided to keep them there for the winter months, during which time the decision was made to embark on the Gallipolli Campaign.

The combined allied landings took place on 25 April, followed by heavy fighting in which Private Richard Read lost his life on 24 May, aged 29.

=====

The 4th Battalion, the Royal Sussex Regiment, including the Arundel Territorials, were also sent to Gallipoli, embarking on the SS Ulysses in July 1915 via a short stopover in Egypt. The Battalion landed at Mudros Bay on 7 August and were fighting in the Battle of Sulva the following day, where two more Arundel men lost their lives. The Battalion stayed in Gallipoli losing many men killed in action, wounded and from illness, before being sent back to Egypt in December.

=====

Arthur Kendall's father, Edward, was a wine cellar man, a trade which Arthur junior took up on leaving school. He was born in Arundel and came from a large family, having six brothers and two sisters, the family growing up in Queens Street. Arthur married Louise in 1907 making their home at 19 Gatwick Terrace, South Marshes, where their daughter Ethel was born. Corporal Kendall served with the 4th Royal Sussex was a very well known citizen and a prominent member of the Arundel Football Club. He was for some time a member of the printing staff of the West Sussex Gazette.

Corporal Arthur Ellis Augustus KENDALL, aged 33, was killed in action at Sulva Bay, just two days after arriving in Gallipolli.

=====

The following day the second Arundel man Private John SILVERLOCK was also killed in action, aged 29. John was the son of George and Sarah and lived at 4 Gatwick Terrace, South Marshes. He had been born at Poling and on leaving school was employed at Constables Brewery as a motor steersman; he had been a Royal Sussex Territorial since 1908.

His mother received a letter from Captain GS Constable following his death;

'I much regret having to write to tell you that your son Jack has been killed in action doing his duty to his Country. Personally I knew him as a soldier and a man who had worked for us for some years, so I feel his loss a great deal, as he was a man to be relied upon to do his duty whatever it was and he was a good soldier. I am glad to say that we were able to bury him decently, the Chaplain conducting the service and his friends have put a cross to mark where he lies'.

=====

On Saturday, 25 September 1915 the 2nd Battalion the Royal Sussex Regiment were ordered to take their positions in the trenches opposite Hulluch and to support both the 1st Loyal Lancashire Regiment and the 2nd Kings Royal Rifle Corps assaulting the German frontline trenches. The action commenced in the early morning with heavy drizzle and a 'veering wind' which blew smoke and gas back towards the British lines, making it impossible for the Royal Sussex to ascertain how the initial attack was progressing. However, they were ordered to advance, but found the enemy wire to be uncut, the first lines of men being mercilessly mown down by the German fire, only a handful surviving. The second line, following up was 'shot to pieces' and every man in the third line were either wounded or killed; by mid afternoon only about seventy men had survived injury or death.

Some 180 Royal Sussex men lost their lives that day including two from Arundel, in one of the bloodiest battles the 2nd Battalion, the Royal Sussex Regiment were involved in.

=====

Private Edward Albert CRANHAM came from a large family. He was born in Thakeham, the third son of farm labourer Frederick and his wife Caroline and had eleven brothers and sisters. His family moved to Arundel and were living at Park Place, when Edward enlisted in the town into the 2nd Battalion, the Royal Sussex Regiment. He died of wounds on 25 September, aged 20

=====

Lance Corporal Percy Frank ROWE was born in Arundel, the son of coal merchant Alfred and his wife, Mary, the family living at 15 Woodview, Ford Road. On leaving school, Percy became an errand boy for a local chemist and then a rural postman, before enlisting in Arundel into the Royal Sussex Regiment in 1905.

Moving to France in August 1914 he fought in the Battle of Marne before being sent home in October suffering from dysentery. It was to be his last home visit. He returned to the Front in December 1914 and fought with them during their battles in 1915 before being killed in action on 25 September 1915, aged 28.

Anxious to obtain more details of his death his family made enquiries via a chum, Private L A Balchin of Bakers Hill, who in turn arranged for a letter to be sent to them from Acting Sergeant Major B Butcher of 'D' Company 2nd Battalion the Royal Sussex Regiment;

'His death was instantaneous being shot through the heart when only a few yards from the enemy's wire. Lance Corporal Rowe was a very popular man with everyone in the Company and always did his duties as a soldier with a cheerful obedience. He was admired for his pluck and daring and was trustworthy to a degree. In losing Lance Corporal Rowe, the Company has lost a comrade and we all send our deepest sympathy to his friends and

relations. He was buried the following morning with some of the others of the Regiment in a soldier's grave in no man's land just north of Veremelles, a short burial service being read over the bodies.
On behalf of 'D' Company please accept our deepest sympathy'.
However, the story does not end there;
'Lance Corporal Percy Rowe's parents have received his pocket book which was picked up on the battlefield and contained a sketch of the young soldier's fiancée. The finder forwarded it to a Hastings newspaper who published a sketch of its interior, including the young lady. By a singular coincidence Percy Rowe's fiancée lived at Hastings and recognised her photograph and was able to recover the lost property. The pocket book also contained a lock of hair in an envelope and a newspaper cutting of his Regiments achievements almost from the outbreak of war, a silent witness to the pride Lance Corporal Rowe had in his Regiment, which had borne the brunt of much heavy fighting with conspicuous gallantry, the last battle in which Lance Corporal Rowe was killed 'being one of their most notable achievements'.

=====

Sergeant Joseph STYLES hailed from Canterbury, Kent, the son of a farm labourer, little has come to light regarding Joseph's early life until he married Lillie in 1900 and moved to Arundel. The couple lived at 22 Kirdford Road, Joseph working until the outbreak of war as a postman in the town.

Joseph enlisted at Lyminster into the 8th Battalion the East Kent Regiment which was raised at Canterbury, as part of Kitcheners Third Army in September 1914 and went to France ten months later. After a long march across part of France they fought in the Battle of Loos and suffered heavy losses, including Sergeant Styles on 26 September, aged 37.

(Sergeant Styles is commemorated on the Memorial Plaque in Arundel Post Office).

=====

1915 HOME FRONT

Early in 1915 the Arundel Soldiers and Sailors Fund was set up to supply local servicemen with extra comforts, sixty three parcels being sent off that month:
'Each parcel contained a waterproof cape, a pack of playing cards, two woollen articles, postcards, pencils in a box of tobacco, a novel and six candles. A similar box was sent to the sailors, except that two pairs of socks were substituted by waterproof capes and chocolate for candles'.
Mr Mills, the Postmaster, promoted the sending of magazines and books to the Front, all these items being much appreciated. An unnamed soldier wrote to the *West Sussex Gazette* thanking the townspeople:

'The people of Arundel in not forgetting their townsmen away, brings back in our more monotonous moments many pleasant memories of days gone by. I am sure that all servicemen belonging to Arundel will appreciate their fellow towns peoples kindly thought of their welfare, comprising as it does comforts while on duty and the means of recreation in their spare time'.

In April the newspaper published an editorial regarding the total number of men having enlisted to date from the Arundel District;

'This ancient town, since the commencement of war, has provided 384 soldiers and sailors for the defence of their Country in their hour of need and must be regarded in every point of view as a splendid effort. For how many other provincial towns can show a finer record or set a commendable example in ready patriotism to the national league'.

Despite the above, the flow of new recruits was dwindling nationally. The Government was aware that close on five million eligible males of military age were not in the forces, of which around one and a half million were in 'starred' or protected jobs and reluctant to introduce compulsory military service, it opted for a half way house scheme devised by Lord Derby. The Derby Scheme informed all men aged 18 to 40 that they could either continue to enlist voluntarily or 'attest', with an obligation to come forward when they were called. Those who attested and were accepted for service, but deferred enlisting until called, were placed in Class A; those who agreed to enlist immediately were placed in Class B. Class A men received one day's Army pay for the day they attested and were issued with a grey armband, sporting a red crown as a sign that they had volunteered. This also avoided any 'white feather' incidents, of which none happened in Arundel, although they did in nearby Bognor. After attestation, Class A men were sent back home to their families and jobs until they were called up.

In the Arundel district 156 men attested of which 42 were rejected for various reasons. A total of 35 men did not attest they were;:

1 discharged soldier
I discharged sailor
1 had died
1 indentured apprentice
8 unfit for examination
2 could not be traced
5 were over age
13 had left town
2 were clergy
1 was required by the police

The Government issued further armbands for those who were either medically unfit for military duty or who had been medically discharged; these men were instructed to apply personally at the Barracks in

Chichester.

Before the canvass the Roll of Honour at the Town Hall contained the names of the men who were serving, however, it took on a different meaning as the casualty lists steadily grew in length.

There were sad farewells when in July, following a short period of home leave, some 150 Arundel Territorials were sent to the new Front at Gallipoli, led by the ex-Mayor, Captain Guy Constable. The Arundel Town Council, at their next meeting, referred to the departure of the local men for foreign service, issuing the following statement:

'That the Town Clerk be asked to convey to the ex-Mayor, Captain Guy Constable and his men of the old 'F' Company, 4th Royal Sussex Regiment and to all the Arundel men serving with the Battalion, the congratulations of the Corporation of Arundel on their proceeding to active service, assuring them that they feel confident that they will faithfully uphold the honour of the County of Sussex and of Arundel and wishing them all good fortune and a safe return'.

One effect of the men departing was causing a problem;

'Our adult population has declined as a consequence of war, but the soldiers have left their dogs behind them, indeed the numbers of dogs seem to be constantly increasing and some of our pavements not infrequently resemble ill swept kennels. Arundel is not as fortunate as Eastbourne, which has a bye-law against barking dogs. We harbour some notorious canine performers whose melodious notes, somewhat restricted in range, raise solos in our streets and duets in half our alleys!'

The nationally introduced lighting restrictions, a safeguard against air raids, necessitated the Arundel tradesmen to close their shops at dusk and the Rifle Club to alter their training schedule from evenings to afternoons. Also, a luminous band was painted around the cavity of the pillar box in Mill Road, 'as residents do not easily find the box in this dark corner'.

Lighting restrictions were relaxed for the winter following discussions in Council and complaints from townsfolk that they could not see to get about in the blackout and several, including a prominent Councillor, having missed their way or got lost, found themselves 'rolling in the gutter'.

Despite the amount of money, presumably saved by the Arundel Gas Company, due to the lighting restrictions, the price of domestic supplies was increased quite sharply by 3d per 1000 cubic feet, 'factors of war time' being given as the reason.

The 'comfortable and admirably equipped little hospital' at St Wilfred's Convent received its first patients in April, when eleven soldiers were sent from the Brighton Eastern General Hospital No 2. The Arundel Voluntary Aid Detachment being mobilised to receive them and ensure that all was ready for their care and comfort;

'Few people, but children saw them come in the early evening, but Arundel is proud to receive them. The services of two trained nurses are provided

through the generosity of the Duchess of Norfolk, whose interest in the Red Cross and nursing work is gratefully acknowledged throughout Sussex'.

The first patients came from the Royal Sussex Regiment, the West Riding Regiment, the Lancashire Regiment and the Black Watch.

Meanwhile the Easter holiday passed quietly;

'There was almost a complete absence of the casual visitors who come to Arundel for fresh air and sunshine. But the presence of the Inns of Court Reserve Corps kept the streets from looking deserted'.

There were other visitors; four Indian Army Officers from Brighton arrived in Arundel on Sunday 28 March, their fine appearance attracting much attention. During their stay they visited the Castle and grounds. The following month 4000 men of 94th Infantry Brigade camped in Arundel Park, where they stayed until June. By the holiday season, however, the grounds were open as usual and more visitors arrived;

'August Bank Holiday under war conditions hardly seemed to a superficial observer to be marked by any great falling off of visitors. Excursionists were naturally fewer than usual, but weekend visitors were very numerous, indeed accommodations were very much taxed. Saturday was one of the busiest days the railway officials at the station have known. Monday was a day of showers, sunshine and boisterous wind, but fortunately the threatening rain did not start in earnest until dusk. The neighbourhood has seldom looked more placidly beautiful than now. The town looked more cheerful and animated on Tuesday than it has yet done this year. It was the first of a series of days when Arundel Castle was open to visitors and there was a great influx of people to profit by the privilege accorded by the Duke and Duchess of Norfolk. Real August weather, bright sunshine after depressing days and pretty frocks made the High Street gay, the Castle grounds looking very green and beautiful'.

Concern was felt throughout the town when His Grace, the Duke of Norfolk was taken ill and underwent an operation in a Leeds hospital. He had been unwell for a little while and it was to be some considerable time before he was able to transact his public business again.

As the summer turned into autumn, news of local casualties from Gallipoli was filtering through involving Arundel's Territorial's as well as others serving with the 2nd Battalion, the Royal Sussex Regiment. The Gallipoli campaign was proving to be a disaster and as Christmas approached the British Forces were being evacuated from Turkey to Egypt.

'Christmas in the town passed very quietly. It was a time of family re-unions, though present conditions had their influence on many of these. The prevalence of khaki in our streets has been an indication of Arundel's generous response to the call of duty. The churches wore their customary Christmas decoration and the services were largely attended'.

The first complete year of the war had ended, a year when another ten men were killed in action and at least ten more were wounded, whilst three became prisoners of war.

1916 WAR FRONT

Mr Edmund and the Honourable Mrs Maxwell-Stuart and family lived at Batworth Park and were totally committed to war service. Father, Private Edmund Maxwell-Stuart, was an active member of the Arundel Volunteer Civil Guard, whilst his daughter was serving as a nurse. There were seven sons, four of whom lost their lives, the first two within six weeks of each other in March and April 1916. They are all commemorated on the Arundel and Lyminster War Memorials; there is a further Special Memorial in Arundel Cathedral.

Lieutenant John Joseph MAXWELL-STUART was serving with the 9th Duke of Wellingtons Regiment. Before the war he had moved to Dorset. He was 19 years old when he was killed in action on 2 March.

Six weeks later, on 26 April Lieutenant Edmund Joseph MAXWELL-STUART, aged 23, was also killed in action:

'Another of the sons of Mr and the Honourable Mrs Maxwell Stuart of Batworth Park, Arundel, has been killed at the Western Front. Lieutenant Edmund Maxwell Stuart, of the Royal Engineers Tunnelling Corps was killed on 26 April in a similar manner and not far from where his younger brother met his death on 2 March'.

The deceased was the third son of his parents. The opinion his comrades had of him is perhaps best expressed by the following extract from a letter received from his Commanding Officer:

"I would have you know that all who knew him admired and loved your son as a fine soldier and true gentleman. His energies were untiring and his conduct exemplary".

In a short space of time two of their sons had been killed in action; two other sons were still serving.

======

Charles Rawlings, the son of carpenter, John and his wife Louisa, was born when the family lived in King Street. He had an older brother, Tom. On leaving school Charles became a gardener, the family then living at River Road from where he enlisted into the Dublin Fusiliers, arriving in France in December 1915. His death four months later was reported in the *Littlehampton Observer*:

'Another of Arundel's sons has fallen in the war. Last week Mrs Rawlings of River Road received intimation that her son Lance Corporal Charles RAWLINGS, aged 24, had been killed in France on 27 April. He had joined the Dublin Fusiliers soon after the outbreak of war. Charlie Rawlings soon gained promotion. He went to France in January 1916 where he met his death. Deep sympathy will be extended to his mother on

the loss of her gallant son'.

On the day of his death, the Dublin Fusiliers suffered heavy casualties during the Battle of Hullach, near Loos, when the Germans attacked them with poison gas.

=====

The Battle of Jutland was the largest naval battle in history, fought over two days, 31 May to 1 June 1916. It had been anticipated since the declaration of war that at some stage the British Grand Fleet and the Imperial German Navy High Seas Fleet would clash. The German Fleet was insufficient in number to engage the entire British Fleet and had planned to lure out, trap and destroy a portion of it, as part of their strategy for breaking the British naval blockade of the North Sea. However, British intelligence had learned that a major naval operation was likely and took the initiative when Vice-Admiral Beatty attacked the German battlecruiser force on 31 May, before their submarine 'pickets' were in position, thus upsetting German plans to divide and conquer the British Fleet.

The two fleets and some 250 ships commenced an epic dual on the afternoon of 31 May, which was to last all night. The result was somewhat inconclusive; the British lost more ships and men whilst the survivor's German surface fleet returned to their home port and were effectively neutralized.

=====

Two Arundel sailors lost their lives in this momentous sea battle:

'The glorious exploits of the Navy in the recent Jutland Bay Battle has added two names to the list of sons who have given their lives for King and Country. The two were very close friends in life and have in death found the same resting place. Leading Signalman Victor WILSON, who was the youngest son of Richard, a naval pensioner, who became Arundel's Recruitment Officer, as well as being a general dealer in his shop at South Marshes. Before enlisting, Victor was an Arundel postman for some years.

Mr and Mrs Wilson and family of South Marshes, wish to thank all friends and neighbours for their kind enquiries and sympathy on the loss of their dear son Victor in the destroyer's night attack in the Battle of Jutland'.

They were not on the same ship; Victor Wilson was serving on the Acasta Class destroyer HMS Fortune, a fairly new vessel, having been launched in March 1913 and allocated to the 4th Destroyer Flotilla. She joined the Grand Fleet at the outbreak of war.

On the night of 1 June, HMS Fortune came under overwhelming fire from German battleships, the guns of one, SMS Westfallen, setting her ablaze and she sank with the loss of 67 crew members. Only one man survived; Victor's body was never found.

=====

'His chum, a former member of the staff of this paper, was serving on board HMS Tipperary, which like HMS Fortune was a Torpedo Boat

Destroyer'.

The eldest son of Claude, a butcher and his wife, Kate, Sick Berth Attendant Reginald D C DALTON was born in Arundel and the family, his two brothers and a sister, lived at 7 Verona Terrace, Ford Road. On leaving school Reginald became a printers apprentice with the *West Sussex Gazette*, before enlisting into the Royal Navy.

His ship, HMS Tipperary, was built along with her three sister ships on the Isle of Wight, fulfilling an order for the Chilean Navy. However, when war was declared the ships were requisitioned by the Royal Navy, completed and put into service.

At the Battle of Jutland, the Tipperary was leading the 4th Flotilla, when they observed a line of ships in the distance, which they were gradually overtaking. Uncertain as to whether they were friend or foe the Tipperary challenged them with her torpedo tubes ready for action. The reply was a rapid and accurate salvo which swept away the bridge, killing the Captain and smothering the ship in flames. Despite this, she still managed to fire her torpedoes before sinking.

There were only twelve survivors from her compliment of 197 men. Some of these, whilst in the Tipperary's Caley Floats, hailed two German 'pulling boats' for help, but were ignored and left to their fate. Reginald's body was washed up on the beach at Egersund, Norway a few days later.

His parents subsequently received the following letter from Norway;

'Mr and Mrs Claude Dalton have received a most kind and sympathetic letter from a Mr and Mrs Staton who live at Egersund in Norway, informing them that the body of their son Reginald, who was on the Tipperary in the Jutland fight, has been washed ashore at Egersund. The kindly inhabitants were able to identify the lad by the letters from home which were found on him. It is some consolation to the bereaved parents to learn that although their son was buried in a strange land, the greatest respect was shown by the inhabitants. Several other bodies washed on the shore were laid to rest at the same time. To quote the letter:

"It was a beautiful funeral with full military honours. The English Consul was present and he spoke with deep emotion on the loss of our brave sailors and expressed sympathy with those at home who had lost their loved ones in the great fight. He also thanked the people of Egersund for their kind and practical sympathy. The coffins were simply covered with wreaths. There were between four and five hundred people present, there has never been such a funeral in Egersund before".

Mr and Mrs Staton concluded their letter by a kindly offering to do anything the parents would like them to do in connection with the tending of the grave and having the lad's name placed thereon. Reginald was aged 23.

=====

The loss of HMS Hampshire accounts for another young Arundel life, that of Stoker First Class Henry Charles KENWARD, aged 21, who was born at Marlborough, Wiltshire, where his father was serving in the Army. The family moved to Arundel in the early 1900s living at Arun Street and held a fine record for patriotic service from the outbreak of war. His father, now demobbed was a National Reservist and Charles' three brothers and a brother in law also answered the Country's call. Before enlisting Charles worked as a general labourer.

Returning to Scapa Flow after fighting at Jutland, HMS Hampshire was immediately withdrawn for a 'diplomatic' mission to Russia. This voyage was 'top secret', as the Hampshire was carrying no less a personage than Lord Kitchener, the British Commander in Chief and Secretary of State for War. At the time it was felt that our Russian allies were 'wavering' and Lord Kitchener's mission was to persuade the Czar and his Generals to remain in the war.

Leaving Scapa Flow and accompanied by two destroyers, HMS Unity and HMS Victor, HMS Hampshire and her escorts ran into a fierce summer storm. Unable to maintain speed, it was thought unlikely there were any enemy submarines in the area and the two destroyers were signalled to return to port, whilst the Hampshire struggled on. At 1940 hrs 'an explosion shook the whole ship'; HMS Hampshire had hit a mine, one of several believed to have been laid by the German submarine U75 prior to the Battle of Jutland and sank within fifteen minutes, taking Lord Kitchener with it.

'Young Kenward went on the Hampshire to the China Station in December 1913 but the ship was recalled at the outbreak of the war. He went on the three weeks trial of HMS Iron Duke and assisted in rescuing the crew of a burning schooner. He also took part in the chase of the Emden and from information to hand evidently participated in the naval battle on 31 May, for a letter from the Engineering Commander of the Hampshire, written a day or two before the Hampshire sank off the Orkneys describes how the Hampshire rammed a German submarine and sank another with gunfire'.

All Arundel will share with these sailors the pride that their glorious deaths inspire'.

(Digressing, further information on this incident was reported in the *Bognor Post* of 14 August 1926 by another Sussex man, Stoker Walter Charles Farnden who lived at Lake Lane, Barnham. He was one of only twelve survivors of HMS Hampshire and his first hand account of the sinking is reproduced here).

'On Saturday 3 June the "Hampshire" steamed into Scapa Flow, was coaled up and moored to a buoy close to the "Iron Duke". On the following Monday, 5 June, Lord Kitchener and his retinue came aboard and orders were given to leave harbour at 5 30pm in the evening. The ship was under sealed orders, but the buzz soon spread to the effect that the destination was to be Archangel. Promptly at 5 30pm the "Hampshire"

slipped her moorings and proceeded out of harbour accompanied by her escorts, the destroyers "Unity" and "Victor". By this time a gale which had prevailed all day had shifted from the north-east to north and was rapidly increasing in violence. The destroyers, almost as soon as they were in the open, found it difficult to keep up with the cruiser in the teeth of the gale and consequently they were ordered to return to port, as they only delayed the "Hampshire".

At 7 30pm I was on watch in the port engine room when a terrific explosion occurred and immediately the ship was plunged into darkness. There was no panic and we all remained at our posts until the order was given to abandon ship. By this time the vessel was down at the bows and was sinking rapidly. When I got on deck Officers and men were standing by their appointed stations. Tremendous seas were running at the time and one boat that I saw lowered from the davits was immediately smashed to pieces against the ship's side. My station was the No 3 Caley Float and after we had assisted in getting the other two floats away we launched our own. There were fifteen or twenty men in the float including myself and by the time we had picked up one or two from the water we were overcrowded. Fortunately for us the current set towards the shore, but it was a terrible ordeal being adrift in those surging seas at the mercy of the wind and waves. About midnight, after four of the most dreadful hours I have ever spent in my life our float was dashed against the rocks near Stromness and a large wave washed me over the side. In the ordinary course of events I cannot swim, but I swam that night and eventually reached a rock and dragged myself ashore. I saw the float again hurled towards the rocks and three of my companions made a jump for it and succeeded in reaching the shore. The remainder were too exhausted to help themselves and perished in the waves when the float overturned. Dazed and shaken I rested awhile, but when I attempted to stand I found that I had lost the use of my legs and I had to crawl until I regained sufficient strength to walk to the nearest cottage. I knocked them up and explained what had happened and they gave me some warm clothing and put me to bed. They afterwards searched the coast and discovered some more survivors. It transpired that six men had been saved from the second float and two from the first making twelve in all.

=====

The blackest day of the Great War for many families in West Sussex was 30 June 1916, when some 360 men of 13th Battalion, the Royal Sussex Regiment, all volunteers and seventeen of their Officers, were killed with a further 1100 men wounded or missing, in the Battle of the Boars Head, which lasted less than five hours.

The Battle of the Boars Head was planned as a diversionary action to make the German High Command believe that this was to be the location of the major offensive planned for 1916, thereby preventing them from moving troops south to the Somme, some fifty kilometres away, where the actual main offensive was to take place. The 11th, 12th & 13th Battalions Royal Sussex Regiment forming the 39th Division were chosen for the attack, the 13th leading, with the 12th on its right and the 11th in reserve.

The attack went ahead in darkness following an artillery bombardment, but soon ran into trouble. Not only were the Germans obviously expecting them, a smoke cloud, designed to mask the British advance, drifted right across the front and made it impossible to see only a few yards ahead, resulting in all sense of direction being lost and devolving the attack into small bodies of men unsure of which way to go.

Some of 11th Battalion in reserve provided stretcher-carrying parties for the 12th and 13th Battalions. The 12th Battalion managed to seize the German front line which they held for four hours against overwhelming German numbers, but lacking reinforcements of both men and ammunition due to enemy action, were forced to withdraw. The 13th Battalion which led the attack were virtually wiped out.

Arundel lost one man killed in the attack (Chichester, Bognor and Littlehampton losing many more), the 30 June becoming known as 'the Day that Sussex Died'.

=====

Private Edward GENT aged 16, was born in Ireland, the family moving to Sussex around 1905, living first at Henfield, before arriving in Arundel, making their home in Gratwicke Terrace. Edward's father, Edmund, had served as a Sergeant in the Royal Sussex Regiment. It seems he probably re-enlisted, because the 1911 Census shows him working as a porter at Arundel Railway Station. Edward enlisted at Worthing into 13th Battalion Royal Sussex Regiment, although clearly underage. He lost his life on 30 June, 'whilst attacking the enemy he was killed by a shell, his death being instantaneous'.

News of his death came via his father, stationed in India, in a 'sympathetic' letter from Colour Sergeant Major C Fowler, who referred to Edward as 'the boy';

'He was practically the youngest soldier in my Company and I can safely say one of the bravest, having not a bit of fear for anything. He was very popular and will be missed'.

=====

The following day, Saturday 1 July, the Somme Offensive commenced. This had been planned following discussions in December 1915, in which the Allies agreed on a concerted offensive against the Germans, of which the Somme Offensive was to be the Anglo-French contribution. Intended to create a rupture in the German line which would be followed by a decisive blow, the Offensive lingered on for the rest of the year. On the first day British and Empire casualties would exceed 57,000, of which over 19000 lost their lives.

======

Sergeant Frederick James STURT, the son of Frederick and Elizabeth Sturt, who lived in Tarrant Street, in the house next door to the Newburgh Arms, was born in Bognor. The family moved to Arundel, where he became a prominent member of the Arundel Football Club. He enlisted into the 2nd Battalion, the Royal Sussex Regiment as a regular soldier and was sent to France in August 1914 where he was wounded at the Battle of Aisne on 14 September, he wrote home to say he was sorry to have 'stopped a bullet' and was now in Southampton Hospital, before being moved.

'For some days he was attended to at the venerable halls of Trinity College, Cambridge which have now been transformed into a hospital. He is now home with his mother in Tarrant Street who tells everybody he went to Cambridge! Mr Sturt takes a graver look at the struggle and thinks that the best German fighters have not been met with yet. He realises that every man is wanted and reports himself as fit at the Chichester Barracks on Friday'.

He returned to the Front only to be gassed in an attack in October 1915.

It was to be a year before his mother received the news that Frederick, aged 30, had been killed in the 'big push' in France. The bad news arrived in Arundel via the priest who was with him when he died of wounds:

'He sent intelligence to a friend in town, who conveyed it to his mother who is now widowed'.

======

It was a 'sympathetic note' from an Officer that informed Thomas Wareham, a domestic gardener and his wife Selina, of Mount Pleasant, of the death of their son Private Herbert Sidney WAREHAM, aged 22, who was one of their seven children.

Herbert enlisted in Kensington into 2/13th Battalion, the London Regiment, which was raised early in September 1914. A Territorial Battalion primarily for home defence, new recruits were trained at the White City. In April 1916 the Battalion was sent to Ireland in response to the Easter Rebellion, but returned after two weeks in preparation for a move to France, which took place on 21 June. Almost immediately the Battalion were in action in the Vimy Sector and it was there on 4 July that Private Herbert Wareham was killed.

Following the official notification of his death the *West Sussex Gazette* commented;

'Herbert is another amongst those from Arundel who have laid down their lives for their Country'.

======

Battery Sergeant Major Harry Joseph CHALLEN LS & GC Medal was the second son of house painter George and Kate Challen of 56 King Street. Harry, who was born and grew up in Arundel, was the husband of Mary and they lived in South Norwood with their two young children. He had been a regular soldier who had completed his service and retired on his Army pension. When war broke out Harry immediately responded to his Country's call and volunteered for service, enlisting in London into the Royal Garrison Artillery. Although offered a home posting as an instructor, this gallant soldier preferred to accompany his Battery to France, taking part in the Battle of Loos and was afterwards sent to the Somme, where his Battery fought in the big offensive. He was almost continually in action until he met his death on 12 August, when an eight inch shell exploded about ten feet away from him. Severely wounded, he was taken to the Casualty Clearing House, where he died from shock a few hours later, aged 39.

Writing to his widow, a fellow Sergeant stated:

'He was the best comrade I ever had; his memory will live on in the hearts of the Officers and men of the Battery, in the working of which he fell so nobly in action'.

The *West Sussex Gazette* concluded;

'The news that Battery Sergeant Major Harry Challen has fallen in action has been received in sorrow by a wide circle of friends in Arundel. He will be remembered by many as a fine example of a British soldier, big, strong and of a very cheery disposition, a keen sportsman and a favourite with all who knew him. He was a capital cricketer and footballer and the town's clubs have often had his useful aid in their matches. The greatest sympathy is extended to his widow and two young children and to his father, mother and brothers in their sad bereavement'.

======

Lieutenant Colonel Edward MOSTYN was the Commanding Officer of the 4th Battalion the Royal Sussex Regiment who because of ill health had to relinquish his command on the eve of the Battalions departure to France. 'D' Company of the 4th Battalion comprised mainly of men from Arundel, Worthing, Littlehampton, Bognor and Chichester and in his memoirs Private R H Sims of Bognor describes the departure of Colonel Mostyn.

'Lieutenant Colonel Mostyn had to relinquish command on account of ill health and declining years and the day before we left for France said goodbye to the Battalion which was drawn up on the Parade Ground at Newhaven under a Battery of guns manned by the Royal Garrison Artillery. This to me as a mere lad of eighteen was by far the most emotional Parade I had to endure in my Service with the Colours. Colonel Mostyn was beloved by all his men and really broke down when he told us he could no longer on account of his declining years take the Battalion overseas and the sad goodbye ended when he wished us all the very best of luck, God Speed and a safe return from the horrors of war. Four hundred and forty seven "Heroes" on that parade never made it, they passed from young lives into eternity that others might live in freedom'.

In July 1916 Lieutenant-Colonel Mostyn 'passed peacefully away' at his home, Tower House, London Road, Arundel, aged 59. He had lived in Arundel for over fifty years and succeeded his late father becoming the agent for the Duke of Norfolk. For many years he had been associated with the 4th Battalion Royal Sussex Regiment 'as a devoted volunteer and convinced Territorial'.

======

Another Arundel NCO, Sergeant Wilfred Bernard GLOSSOP, serving with a heavy battery of the Royal Garrison Artillery, died of wounds on 19 August, age unknown. Wilfred, the son of a local Councillor, was born and enlisted at Arundel. At its monthly meeting, the Arundel Council passed a vote of sympathy, commiserating with Councillor WE Glossop in the death in action of his son. The Mayor said he hoped the sad hour would be brightened for the parents, by the knowledge of the fact that their son died fighting for his King and Country.

'Much sympathy has been extended to Mr and Mrs WE Glossop in the loss sustained by the death of their youngest son, Sergeant Wilfred Glossop, of the Royal Artillery, who was killed in France quite recently. Details of how he met his death are not yet to hand. Bernard, as he was familiarly known in Arundel, has been in the Army for twelve years. He was formerly on the staff of the Arundel Post Office. He leaves a widow and three small children who are living in Queenstown, Ireland. It is a sad memory for many that Mr and Mrs Glossop lost their eldest son in the Boer War'.

======

The death of Private Wilfred SCUTT, MM, aged 22 was not reported in the West Sussex Gazette until March 1917, although it had occurred on 15 September 1916, on the Somme:

'Wilfred was the son of Private Charles Scutt (RDC) and Mrs Scutt of 88 Surrey Street. He went out to Canada nearly five years ago and upon the outbreak of war joined the Canadian contingent. After a period of training he went to France in 1915 and saw much fighting. To his high character, his Officers have paid tribute and that his courage has been recognised affords comfort and pride to his parents'.

The wait for news must have been agonising for his parents.

His Military Medal was also awarded in March 1917.

'The Military Medal for bravery in the field has been awarded to Private Wilfred Charles Scutt, who was killed in the Battle of the Somme on 15 September last'..

======

Mr and Mrs Frank Jones were in a similar position. Their son Private Cyril Frank JONES had been missing for some months:

'Mr and Mrs Frank Jones of Commerce House have received intimation from the CO that their son, Cyril Jones, has been missing since 30 September. Although he is still in his teens he has served his Country since

the outbreak of war, having put on his age to join the Motor Section of the Kent Cycle Battalion as a despatch rider. In July he was hastily sent to France and there attached to the 7th Buffs. Mr and Mrs Jones wish to thank all those who have shown them much kindness during the suspense through which they are passing'

Eventually the news they feared was confirmed, their son, Private Cyril Jones had been killed in action on 30 September, aged 19.

=====

Arundel's oldest serving casualty was Private George GOATCHER, who was born in Berkshire. His family had at one time lived in Arundel and had moved back to the town by 1861. They lived in Maltravers Street, his father employed as a servant/groom. Both George's parents had passed away by the time George had left school and he was working as a printer's compositor. He was by now the head of the family before meeting and marrying his wife, Emily.

Private George Goatcher enlisted into the Labour Company of the Royal Army Service Corps and 'died' in France on 29 November 1916, aged 59. No further details are to hand.

=====

Another older man serving was Private James William KENWARD who first joined the Royal Sussex Regiment at an early age and served for fifteen years, holding both the Egyptian Medal & Star and the North-West Frontier Medal. He retired in 1901, but answered his Country's call at the outbreak of war, enlisting into the Home Reserve Battalion of the Royal Sussex Regiment.

In October 1916 he was stationed at Colchester, Essex, employed in the hazardous task of loading bombs into boxes ready for sending to the Front, this activity taking place in a shed. Approximately one hundred yards away some soldiers were engaged in test firing bombs by throwing them from a trench into a crater, when a fragment of one of them flew across to the shed in which Private Kenward was working and entered through an existing aperture in the gable end and hitting him behind his right ear. A Doctor was immediately summoned who stopped the bleeding and the wound subsequently healed. However, a few days later Private Kenward suffered a serious internal bleeding which led to his death.

The accident was caused by a combination of several factors. Firstly the fallout from the bombs rarely travelled more than twenty five yards, but this one travelled four times that distance. Secondly, the shrapnel did not make a hole in the side of the shed in which Private Kenward was working, but flew cleanly through 'a small aperture' already existing and thirdly Private Kenward just happened to be in its way at that particular moment. Subsequent X Rays revealed that a small piece of shrapnel had lodged near the base of Private Kenward's skull.

His body was brought back to his home at 19 Arun Street, Arundel for burial, the chief mourners being his wife, Elizabeth, his daughter, Catherine and his two sons, 1st Class Stoker James W Kenward, serving in HM Submarine J3 and Drummer Ernest George Kenward, of the Royal Sussex Regiment; only a few months earlier his third son, 1st Class Stoker Henry Charles Kenward, had been lost on HMS Hampshire.

Many townsfolk attended the funeral, including the Mayor of Arundel, Councillor Herbert Dorman. His coffin was borne from Arun Street to the Cemetery by members of the RDC, the Arundel Volunteers fired three volleys at the graveside and the Last Post was sounded by Bandsman A Elms, late of the Royal Sussex Regiment. Private James William Kenward was aged 50.

=====

1916 HOME FRONT

With many men away fighting, the manpower shortage was beginning to show:

'On and from Monday next, 13 March, the Arundel Head Post Office will be open for public business between the hours of 9am and 12 noon and 2pm and 7pm only. Exceptionally, telegrams may be handed in at the Sorting Office door between noon and 2pm., and telegrams will be delivered as usual during these hours. The hours of attendance at the Tortington Post Office in Ford Road will be identical. The changes have been decided upon in consequence of depletion of staff and the insistent need for economy. It is felt by the State that the public will cheerfully assist by transacting their Post Office business as early in the day as possible and especially by posting their letters during the morning or early afternoon, whenever practicable. Arundel is not singular in this curtailment of facilities'.

Food was becoming in short supply by April. With the Country having only about six weeks of wheat reserve left, the Arundel bakers announced that, owing to this shortage, they would not be making any hot cross buns this year!

Moves had been started to organise a Women's Land Army, the Government wanting woman to get involved in the production of food as their contribution to the war effort. A recruitment meeting was held at the Castle:

'Really wonderful work is being done by women', declared the Countess of March, who presided at a well attended meeting to promote their work on the land, which by the kindness of the Duke and Duchess of Norfolk was held in the Baron's Hall of the Castle on Saturday evening'.

A very good start had been made in Sussex and it was hoped that, as a result of this meeting, many more women would come forward to work on the land, thereby giving valuable service to the Country. The fact that some of them had not registered themselves because they thought they might be compelled to work in the next village or some distant village, led the Countess to declare emphatically that;

There is nothing of the nature of compulsion in the scheme. Women can assist either in unskilled or casual work, or as skilled whole time workers, who were naturally the more important. To those who took up the latter three months training would be given. There was no end to the things which women could do on the land to assist the farmers who are so short of labour. It was really useful war work, they would like the outdoor life but they must not be afraid of hard work and women of the upper classes must set a good example. By taking the places of milkers, cowmen, stockmen and other skilled hands on farms they would be helping to win the war. On one farm a woman is rearing 45 calves and 40 pigs.'

The price of milk was also causing concern, being raised by a penny a quart later in the year before reverting to the original price. The *West Sussex Gazette* sent 'their man' to investigate:

'Much relieved were local milk vendors on Saturday when it became known from an announcement in the press that further orders relating to the price of milk had been made. These included the removal of the proviso limiting the price to be charged so that it cannot exceed the price at November 15. Subsequent to that date the price locally was advanced from 5d to 6d, with the possibility of dire penalties falling upon the dealers. Our representative inquiring from one of the vendors was introduced to his wife who had just returned from a long milk round in the keen frost, in her pony and cart, who remarked to her husband:

"Perhaps if that newspaper fellow had been on my job this morning he would have thought the price of milk ought to be 1s a quart!"

The Arundel Work Depot announced that it had received another contract from the Government to make hospital shirts from Government flannel and appealed to the townsfolk for donations to help buy materials. Over the previous six months the ladies had made over one thousand items ranging from bed socks to operation stockings.

Much time was spent entertaining the many wounded soldiers recuperating in the town;

'No effort is spared to give the wounded soldiers at the local Red Cross Hospital a good time and the men are not slow to show their appreciation, fortnightly concerts are held and are always very enjoyable. Then there are drives, river trips and picnics and last but not least stoolball matches, in which the soldiers seemed to revel. Recently the local ladies club entertained them on the Waterwood Plain, to a match and tea. Then on Tuesday last the return was played. On this occasion the sister in charge was the hostess, who not only entertained the rival teams, but also all the helpers at the hospital. Consequently there was a merry party of over sixty

and tea in real picnic style was much enjoyed. The wounded made a good match of it and scored 63 runs, of which Private Harding made 18. The stoolball club's score however, was 96'.

Not only resident wounded soldiers were entertained; in August 1916 visiting wounded soldiers were entertained at Arundel Castle:

'There was very much that was significant of English life at its best in the gathering which lifted Arundel Castle and its grounds into Imperial usefulness and prominence on Monday afternoon, when their Graces entertained about 700 wounded soldiers from hospitals in West Sussex.

Their guests were brought hither and thither by their arrangement, chiefly in the swift open modern vehicles which allow folk to see the countryside as a panorama passing before them. Entering by the Mill Lodge, from the valley level itself, the guests, many of them it must be borne in mind, the cream of the young men of the Country of all classes, were met by their hosts in the Baron's Hall. If they so wished they made their way to the private grounds, where, under a summer sun they found rest, refreshment, music, singing and the attendance of a group of people, who gladly accepted the invitation of the Duke and Duchess to come and help entertain "our friends". There were many among that tired, maimed, but delighted throng, to whom the visit itself, socially and scenically, must have been a revelation.

The afternoon included entertainment by the Band of the Royal Marine Artillery, (Portsmouth), the choir of St Philip's Church and refreshments including a tea. The soldiers left in the late afternoon and were cheered as they drove out of town by the townspeople.'

Other visitors in 1916 including key war workers:

'The town wore quite a pre-war aspect on Saturday when two well laden char-a-bancs set down a gay party of holiday makers. They were employees at the Hendon Aerodrome, who, having had a very strenuous time of late, had chosen a trip by road to Arundel. Fine weather favoured a delightful run and the enjoyment of the trippers was enhanced by the fare provided at the luncheon and tea at the Norfolk Hotel'.

However, news from the war was bad. The year had seen the biggest naval engagement of the war at Jutland, where two local sailors were lost, with another going down on HMS Hampshire with Lord Kitchener two weeks later. The Battle of the Somme, heralded by an action involving the Royal Sussex Regiment at the Boars Head and other incidents accounted for another nine men and many more were wounded.

Arundel's Doctor Butcher applied to the Council to be released to join the Royal Medical Corps. The Council passed a resolution expressing the opinion that his services could not be spared, as he had a very large area to cover and he was also doing half the work of another Doctor who had joined the Corps.

A Christmas Day collection by Arundel children for the starving children of Belgium raised £19 15s 03/4d

=====

1917 WAR FRONT

Lance Corporal Leo Lawrence QUINTON was born in Arundel, where his father, Charles worked as a draper's assistant, in a premises next door to the London and County Bank, in the High Street. His mother, Anne, ran a boarding house. The family had moved from Arundel before the war, whilst Leo who had been at boarding school in Middlesex had enlisted into the 10th Battalion, the Middlesex Regiment. He later served with the 5th East Kent Regiment and was killed in action on 18 January 1917, aged 20, whilst serving in Iraq.

=====

Having withdrawn from Gallipoli at the end of 1915 the 4th Battalion, the Royal Sussex Regiment had remained in Egypt around the Suez area. In 1917 they became part of the Egyptian Expeditionary Force sent to dislodge the Turkish forces from the series of ridges they held between Gaza and Beersheba, thereby opening the way to Palestine, this became known as the First Battle of Gaza.

Although numerically superior, the task was a difficult one, the British attack being launched on 26 March, advancing under the protection of a dense sea fog. The attack was led by the Cavalry with the Infantry following, advancing across difficult terrain. A misunderstanding at Command level led the British to withdraw the Cavalry, under the impression that the Infantry attack had failed. In fact, a British victory was on the cards; even the German commander of the Turkish forces thought the day had been lost. The British attack resumed the following day, by which time the Turks had reinforced their positions and the Battle ended in a costly stalemate. Some 4000 British soldiers were wounded or killed in action.

'It was expected that the toll of casualties in the Palestine fighting would include some of our local lads, seeing that the 4th Royal Sussex Regiment were so heavily engaged there',

Captain Constable, was awarded the Military Cross for his actions in the attack, during which he was wounded, but able to continue with his duties; whilst six of his fellow Arundelians lost their lives.

=====

An Arundel lad born and bred, Private Walter John BUCK lived at Rookes Cottages, Chichester Road, before moving to The Lodge, Swanbourne Lake. The son of bricklayer George Buck and his wife Fanny, Walter was employed as an under cowman at a private dairy in Arundel. Like many other Arundel lads he enlisted in the early days of the war and made the

---

journey to the railway station, perhaps taking a last look across the water meadows at his home town as the train took him to war.

He had enlisted into the 4th Battalion, the Royal Sussex Regiment and served with them through the Gallipoli campaign. After that the Battalion found themselves in Gaza fighting fierce battles with the Turks. It was during the first of these that Walter lost his life on 25 March, aged 27. His death was not immediately confirmed, Walter being reported as missing initially, confirmation reached his family in Arundel in July 1917.

======

Sergeant William Joseph AYLING was born in the hamlet of South Stoke and was killed in action on 26 March, at the First Battle of Gaza, aged 37.

'One of several gallant Arundelians who have made the supreme sacrifice is Sergeant William Joseph AYLING, the husband of Mrs W Ayling, of 87 Surrey Street, who was most highly esteemed by all who knew him. He was a Territorial, who was formerly employed in the saw mills on the Duke of Norfolk's Estate. Much sympathy is felt for his devoted wife and two children'.

In a personal tribute to him, Sergeant W Hersee, who was injured in the same action wrote;

'Sergeant Ayling lost his life, falling as he lived, a splendid example of a soldier and man'.

They had been great chums all the three years of military service they had seen together.

======

After months of anxiety, the parents of two Arundel lads, who were reported missing in the first attack on Gaza on 26 March 1917, received the official notification that their sons had been killed in action, fifteen months later, in July 1918.

Private Reginald KERR the son of Mrs Kerr of 7 River Road, Arundel, was born in Brighton, where his father worked as a tailor. Within a year or so the family had moved to Causeway Cottages, Lyminster and by 1911 to Arundel, by which time Reginald's father had passed away. Before enlisting Reginald worked as an errand boy as well as joining the Territorial's.

======

The second soldier was Private Victor STAMP the son of Mr and Mrs Stamp of Park Place, Arundel. Both soldiers were 21 years old.

'Mr and Mrs WJ Stamp were notified in November 1917 that their son Private A J Victor Stamp had been killed sometime earlier in the first Battle of Gaza'.

======

There has been a butchers shop in Arundel High Street in the hands of the Read family since before 1881. Owned by Richard Read and his wife Rosetta the family had four children of whom one of them, Charles, (the brother of Richard, see 1915) enlisted into the Royal Sussex Regiment. A butcher's assistant on leaving school he was well known in Arundel as a 'clever forward in the Arundel Town Football Club'. Charles married his wife, an Arundel lass Charlotte, in 1908 and by the time of his death in the Battle of Gaza they had four young children living with them in their home 4 River Road. Private Charles Henry READ was killed in action on 26 March, aged 28.

======

Company Sergeant Major George Francis WELLER was another of Arundel's Royal Sussex sons, who was well known and much liked, to have been killed in action in the fighting in Palestine, aged 34. Born in Warningcamp, George, a single man, who had recently lived in Littlehampton where his mother received the sad news of his death. George was still residing in Littlehampton but most of his days were spent in Arundel, where he was a member of the Bellringers Association and of the Parish Church Choir. He was afterwards in a choir at Littlehampton.

======

An apprentice grocer on leaving school, Private Arthur WEST lived with his widowed mother, Kate and was the middle one of three sons. The family lived at 9 South Marshes, Arundel. Arthur enlisted into the 4th Battalion, the Royal Sussex Regiment at Littlehampton. It seems this may have been because he was clearly underage and perhaps he had less chance of being caught enlisting in another town where he was not known. The 1911 Census gives his age as 9 years old. His date of death, 26 March 1917 was only six years later. So if the Census was correct, Arthur was only 15 years old when he was killed in action.

======

The Second Battle of Gaza was the second British attempt to force their way through the Turkish lines. Preparations for this attack were intensive, including the construction of a railway, the digging of several large reservoirs and the positioning of ammunition dumps. However, during the intervening three weeks, Gaza had also been strongly reinforced and garrisoned.
This Battle commenced on 17 April with the numerically stronger British forces supported by eight tanks, twenty five aircraft, a French destroyer and two British monitors.
The attack was a total failure costing 6444 British casualties: the Turkish losses were much lower.

======

Serving with the 4th Battalion, the Royal Sussex Regiment and a survivor of the First Battle of Gaza was Sergeant William CLEMENTS. William was born in Worcestershire, where he still lived in the early 1900s employed as a carpet weaver. When he moved to Arundel is not known, but by 1911 he was married to Sarah, whose parents ran the Abercrombie

Inn, in Queen Street, the pair making their home next door in Abercrombie Cottage. William was now employed by the General Post Office in Arundel, where he was a Postal Telegraph Foreman, volunteering for service at the outbreak of war. He was killed in action on 19 April 1917, aged 38. This was the first day of the Second Battle of Gaza, which cost the lives of over five hundred men in his Division.

'Deep sympathy is felt for Mrs Clements who has received official notification of the death in action of her husband Sergeant William Clements serving with the Royal Sussex in Egypt'.

======

The Third Battle of Gaza was launched on 31 October 1917 when the British Infantry attacked Beersheba. Backed up by the Desert Mounted Corps, Beersheba was finally taken following a Cavalry charge by the Australian 4th Light Horse Brigade against the Turkish positions. Operations against Gaza commenced on 2 November with a night attack along the coast. The British advanced two miles and held their positions until a further assault commenced on 6 November.

======

Two Arundel lads serving with the 4th Battalion, the Royal Sussex Regiment were killed in action in Palestine. Private Charles MERRYDEW, aged 29, was one of fourteen children born to Charles, a groom/coachman and his wife, Jane. Charles was born in Tortington the family living in Woodview and later in Kirdford Road. On leaving school Charles worked as a cowman on a dairy farm, but shortly before the war moved to Broadwater, Worthing and enlisted at Newhaven. His death came just six months after his younger brother, Harry, had lost his life.

'The first positive news of the death of a member of the staff of the West Sussex Gazette on any Front reached us on Thursday, when we learnt that Private Harry Merrydew of the 13 Royal Sussex Regiment, formerly an apprentice of ours who volunteered, had been killed in France on 13 March. He had been out about six months and his mother, who lives at Broadwater now, has received his pocket book and a kind letter from Captain H H Story who says that Merrydew "was a capable and reliable machine gunner who was sitting in a dug-out in the trenches when a shell got a direct hit. He was taken back that night and buried this morning. Your boy died a soldier, doing and having done his bit".

======

Lance Corporal Archibald Edmund (Teddy) TESTER, MM aged 29 of River Road, also serving with the 4th Battalion, the Royal Sussex Regiment succumbed to his severe wounds received the previous day, on 7 November. Born in Arundel, he was the only child of George and Sarah and before enlisting in Horsham was actively involved with the Arundel Football Club. Only four months earlier his parents had been notified that Archibald had been awarded the Military Medal for 'conspicuous gallantry', a medal they received a few weeks after his death.

=====

Private EP STONE of the 4th Royal Sussex was also killed in action in 1917 but no details of him have come to light. There were several families of that surname in Arundel but so far this man has not been traced. His name does not appear on the War Memorial.

=====

Born in Brighton, Private Arnold H CROWTHER may have lived in Shropshire for a while before moving to Arundel, where he also enlisted. His first spell of service was as a Trooper with the Sussex Yeomanry, after which he transferred into the 10th Battalion, the Royal West Kent Regiment. He was killed in action on 24 February, aged 24.

=====

Lance Sergeant George Joseph COOK was born in Yorkshire. He came from a large family, his father, Frederick was a gardener, whilst his mother was busily engaged looking after her seven children. When he started work George followed his father also becoming a gardener, leaving home to work at the Brigstock Manor House in Northamptonshire. It is not known when or what bought him to Arundel, however, it was here that he enlisted into the Royal Sussex Regiment, before joining the 2nd Battalion, the Royal West Surrey Regiment. He died of wounds on 27 April, aged 27.

=====

The Second Battle of Arras was fought over a five week period form 9 April, which was Easter Sunday, until 16 May and was a major British offensive. The 7th Battalion, the Royal Sussex Regiment were involved from the start, going over the top at 05 30am. Initially all went well, the German front line trench being captured within a hour or two. The planners had decreed that the men were to then re-organise and consolidate their positions, whilst a British artillery barrage paved the way forward. Sadly the barrage fell short of their target leaving the next line of German defenders virtually intact. This resulted in a heavy loss of life as the Royal Sussex went forward, unaware of the failure of the artillery barrage, the German riflemen and machine gunners inflicting a heavy toll.

=====

Private Leonard Daniel WOOD lost his life in that day in the advance, aged 27. Born in Arundel, one of nine children, Leonard, the second son, worked as a milkman for a private dairy prior to enlisting at Woking into the 7th Battalion, the Royal Sussex Regiment.

=====

For some unknown reason the name of Private John HUDSON is omitted from the Arundel War Memorial, although he was born and lived all his life in the town, firstly in Maltravers Street, before the family moved to Bond Street, During these years his father, William worked as a journeyman carpenter and a groom. In the years leading up to the Great

War, John was employed as a draper's assistant, by Messrs Harvey Nicholls and Company, in Knightsbridge. John was killed in action on 14 April, aged 35.

=====

Another member of the West Sussex Gazette staff to lose his life was Private Henry Joseph COLEMAN the son of stonemason Harry and his wife, Elizabeth, who lived for many years at California Terrace, Tortington, before moving to 59 Tarrant Street, Arundel. Henry enlisted at Littlehampton into the 1st Battalion, the East Kent Regiment, being killed in action on 15 April.

Mrs Coleman received a 'very kind' letter from the Adjutant of the 1st Battalion the Buffs sympathising with her on the death of her son;

'With the fearless and faithful manner in which he discharged his duties and his unwearied cheerfulness and soldierly qualities, the Regiment was proud to possess one who so steadily upheld its finest traditions and one who enjoyed the warm affection of his comrades'.

=====

Also reported killed in action in April 1917 was H STERRY of the Royal Fusiliers, but no other information is to hand.

=====

Private Charles Henry ROGERS appears on the Arundel War Memorial as well as Lyminster's, living as he did at The Bungalow, Warningcamp. A former member of the Red Cross, Charles had been an employee of Messrs Constable and Son. Married to Alice, Charles had one child. Formerly with the Royal Sussex Regiment he was serving with the Machine Gun Corps and had only been at the Front for three weeks when he was killed in action on 6 May.

=====

Private Reginald PRANGLE probably lived in Arun Street and served with the Royal West Surrey Regiment died aged 18. Whether this was from wounds or illness has not been established.

=====

The Royal Defence Corps was formed in 1917, converting the existing Home Service Garrison Battalions into a more organised structure, on the lines of Infantry Regiments. It was composed of men who for reasons of age or health were unable to perform front line service. The duties of the Royal Defence Corps were varied and centred at home, guarding railway lines, military installations, prisoners of war etc.

=====

Sergeant Charles Thomas SLAUGHTER aged 58, may have lived at 46 King Street and was a time expired Royal Sussex man who had originally enlisted at Middleton many years earlier. With the outbreak of war he re-enlisted at Arundel and died at home on 16 May 1917.

=====

The sad news of the death of Trooper Laurie RATLEY aged 28 was received 'with the greatest regret by his friends in the town' and much sympathy was felt for his young wife and child. Laurie was born and enlisted in Arundel and was formerly a member of the Local Volunteers. He had been with the Colours barely six months and had been in France but a few weeks before receiving the wounds which led to his death in a Base Hospital. Previous to joining the Army he was an esteemed employee of Messrs Lambert and Norris.

The Household Battalion were engaged in operations against well defended German positions in the Fampoux area at the time Trooper Ratley was wounded.

'Mrs Ratley wishes to thank all kind friends for their sympathy in the loss of her dear husband'.

======

Private Alfred Charles GARDNER was over military age when the war broke out, but 'patriotically volunteered for service', joining the Army Veterinary Corps. He was the son of Charles and Emma Gardner and had been born in Arundel, although he enlisted in Brighton. Prior to enlisting he was employed as a house painter and lived in Park Place with his wife, Sarah and their five children. Aged 47, he became ill, whilst in France, with Lobular Pneumonia which took his life on 8 June 1917.

======

Private Frederick SWAIN was from a well known family in Arundel due to his father's employment as the local Pearl Assurance Agent. Through this position he would have known many families and fellow soldiers in the days before they enlisted. Frederick was born in Arundel and also joined the Company, at one time working in Cambridge, the home town of his wife, Elizabeth, where they lived with their young son, Walter. They then moved to Westminster where Frederick enlisted at Whitehall into the London Regiment. On 16 June 1917, Frederick was killed in action, aged 40.

======

On 19 June 1917 Lance Corporal Reginald John COLEMAN, aged 29, serving with the Machine Gun Corps, was killed in action. His late father had been a Builders Manager, the family living in Queen Street, Arundel, when Reginald was a child. Reginald's name does not appear on the Arundel War Memorial.

======

'The Secretary of the Admiralty regrets to report that HMS Vanguard blew up whilst at anchor at Scapa Flow as a result of an internal explosion. The ship sank immediately and there were only three survivors among those on board the ship at the time of the disaster, one Officer and two men, the Officer has since died. There were, however, twenty four Officers and seventy one men not on board the ship at the time, thus bringing the total

number of survivors up to ninety seven'.

======

Ordinary Seaman Ernest James CARVER the son of James lived at Bakers Hill, Arundel and was one of the unlucky men to still be aboard the Vanguard when she blew up at Scapa Flow on 9 July 1917. He was 18 years old.

======

A member of a family well known and esteemed in Arundel, Bombardier Harry PECKHAM lost his life on the Belgium frontier. He joined the Royal Field Artillery in October 1914 and went to the Front in March 1915 and with the exception of two ten days leaves had been there ever since. On the 17 July some bales of hay fell on him while he was sleeping, severely injuring his liver. An operation was successfully performed at No 3 Canadian Casualty Clearing Station and he appeared to be going on favourably, but two days later he became worse and passed peacefully away, aged 47.

He was married to Clara and was the second son of the late Mr Harry Peckham of 157 Kings Street. When at Arundel he was a member of the Parish Choir.

======

Lance Corporal Charles George DENYER the son of George and Annie of Eagle House, Maltravers Street, was born and enlisted into the 7th Battalion, the Royal Sussex Regiment in Arundel. He was the husband of Lillian who came from Bracknell in Buckinghamshire.

On the 25 July 1917, the 7th Battalion were occupying trenches, resting and providing working parties when the Germans made a surprise attack, using trench mortars, bombs and flame and gas throwers. Strategically the trenches that the 7th Sussex had to vacate were not of great importance, but the lives of the twenty two men lost, was a great blow. It was to be nearly a year, August 1918, before Lillian received news of his death;

'Lance Corporal CG Denyer, the son of Mr and Mrs George Denyer of Maltravers Street, was reported as missing on 25 July 1917 and although every effort has been made to obtain information respecting him, nothing was heard until a few days ago, when his young wife received official notification that her husband was killed. Charlie Denyer was one of four brothers all on active service'.

======

Second Lieutenant William Henry GUNNER MC was the son of Mr and Mrs WH Gunner, of Bank House, High Street, Arundel, his father being the manager of the London County and Westminster Bank. A member of the Arundel football team, William enlisted and in April 1917, received his commission in the Royal Flying Corps Military Wing.

Flying with 60 Squadron, he did not take long to make an impact, as reported in early July 1917;

'An award which will cause gratification in the Borough is that of the Military Cross to Second Lieutenant W H Gunner of the Royal Flying Corps. The official reason for the award is not yet disclosed, but details have already been received of an exciting adventure for the recipient during operations in France. A shot fired at him ricocheted from his machine gun and wounded him in the head. His machine dive nosed down for about 3000 feet but the gallant Officer recovered in time to right matters and land safely. The relatives of the honoured soldier have received many messages of congratulations'.

A day or so later William was again in action;

'While on offensive patrol he engaged and attacked nine hostile aircraft, two of which were attacking the rear machine of his patrol. Having conveyed the other machine back to the aerodrome he again returned with his patrol in response to an urgent call for aeroplanes to drive off hostile aircraft. He had been wounded in the previous encounter but insisted on carrying on and on numerous other occasions he has shown great skill and courage in offensive work'.

For this he was awarded the Military Cross.

The life expectancy of a Royal Flying Corps pilot could be measured in days and William was soon to lose his. Whilst flying an SE 5 on 29 July he failed to return from a sortie;

'No tidings have yet been received of Second Lieutenant William Gunner, General List and Royal Flying Corps, who was reported as missing on the 29 July. Only recently as reported in our columns His Majesty the King was pleased to confer on him the Military Cross for "Bravery and Skill against hostile aircraft". Warm sympathy will be felt for his parents Mr and Mrs WH Gunner and family in their anxiety'.

It was to be another four weeks before news of William's fate became known, believed killed in action on 29 July, aged 26.

'Very great sympathy will be felt with Mr and Mrs WH Gunner who have received official information from the Military Secretary of the Secretary of State, as to the fate-although this is not yet certain- of his son Second Lieutenant William Gunner MC, General List and Royal Flying Corps. The War Office communicate an entry from the NOEDDUETSCHE ALLGEMEINE ZEITUNG of 18 August which records the fall into German hands of Lieutenant Gunner's one seat machine, in circumstances which suggest it was fired when he was in the air during the fighting. When he was last observed he was above a formation of enemy scouts, too far over to be seen from the British lines. The German information is considered to be correct, but will not be accepted officially until after the lapse of a rather longer period. The Squadron Captain says;

"Your son was a good fellow and a splendid fighter and he could always be relied upon in a fight and was consequently a great favourite in the Squadron".

(In 1918, in the presence of the Officers and men of the Royal Sussex Regiment at Chichester Barracks, Lieutenant Colonel HR Lloyd publicly presented to Mr WH Gunner, of Bank House, Arundel, the Military Cross won by his son, the late Second Lieutenant WH Gunner, of the Royal Flying Corps).

=====

At dawn on 31 July 1917, the 11th, 12th and 13th Battalions of the Royal Sussex Regiment went over the top together as part of the Third Battle of Ypres also known as Passchendaele. This was to prove to be the most horrific battle of the war and lasted three months; by the end of the first day over one hundred Sussex boys had lost their lives. As the days wore on casualties continued to mount and the ground became an absolute quagmire as heavy rains set in. The battlefield began to flood, as the troops got bogged down in the mud, in the face of heavy enemy shelling, mortars, rifle and machine gun fire.

=====

Arundel lost two men at Passenchdaele, both ex employees of the *West Sussex Gazette*. Lance Corporal Benjamin AYLING, aged 31, who was serving with the 13th Battalion the Royal Sussex Regiment was the son of Ben and Anne Ayling and husband of Minnie Gladys Ayling, 7 Wood View, Ford Row. Benjamin was born in Arundel and worked at the Horsham Branch of the newspaper, 'but returned to Arundel, whence he readily responded to his Country's call'
'Deep sympathy is felt for Mrs Minnie Ayling of Wood View, Ford Road, whose husband, Corporal Benjamin Ayling of the Royal Sussex Regiment was killed in action on 31 July, also his bereaved parents at Offham. On the date mentioned he was reported as missing, but his widow has now heard from the War Office of his death.

=====

Lance Corporal Wilfred BUDD, aged 28, also served with the 13th Battalion. In a letter expressing sympathy with Mrs Budd, of 67 Maltravers Street in the loss of her son, his Platoon Commanding Officer says;
'At the beginning of the big advance we were crossing No Man's Land in the very first wave of the advance when he was struck by a bullet. He died instantaneously and I believe painlessly. Later in the day we went back and buried him where he fell with a number of others from our Company. Personally I thought a great deal of him and he will be a great loss to us all. He was one of the best NSO's always cheerful and keen at his work under the most trying conditions and he died like a brave man at the front of the attack. Please accept my deepest sympathy with you in your loss'.
Before enlisting Wilfred had been employed by the West Sussex Gazette;
'The inhabitants of Arundel will feel deeply for the bereaved family, for Lance Corporal Budd was well known and well liked. He had long been employed by us and at the time he answered his Country's call was a

member of our clerical staff. He was a pleasing vocalist and a Chorister at St Philip Nero'.

Lance Corporal Budd had been wounded in October 1916 and spent four months back in Arundel recovering; returning to his Regiment in January 1917.

=====

At the end of August the 13th Battalion, the Royal Sussex Regiment were back in the Ypres area after a period of rest and relaxation, where Corporal Walter Joseph GLOSSOP, aged 28, lost his life;

'Deep sympathy is felt for Councillor WE Glossop and Mrs Glossop in the loss of their son, Corporal Walter Glossop of the Royal Sussex Regiment who was killed in action on the night of 28/29 August. In a letter of sympathy to his parents Second Lieutenant RG Hollingham writes;

"We were relieving another Battalion in the Front Line and just as your son had taken over his post with his team a shell burst just in front of the parapet. He fell down and when we reached him we found he was dead. I, as your son's Platoon Commander found him one of the best types of soldier, willing, obedient and smart, both in character and work and I feel his loss keenly. The very night of his death I had him promoted to Corporal and I can safely say it would not have been long before he was made Sergeant, although I believe he was not keen on taking stripes, he was very reserved. As no doubt you know he was a Lewis gunner and thoroughly knew his gun. He always looked after it and not once did I find his gun dirty or out of order. Corporal Glossop was a man who could be trusted and one in whom I could rely".

His Company Sergeant Major HW Cheal also wrote;

'Your son, Corporal Glossop joined at about the same time as myself three years ago and we have always been in the same Company. Poor Walter, he was indeed one of the best of our original boys of whom, alas, very few are left. He was always the same old cheery sort, never downhearted and thoroughly reliable in every corner, no matter how tight. We all miss him very much and we all assure you of our deep sympathy in your sad loss'.

Walter Glossop's grandparents were 'mine hosts' at the Old Ship in King Street, where Walter had worked as an assistant barman. Born in Arundel, Walter enlisted in the town. He was wounded in August 1916 and was home on leave about six weeks earlier. Before the war he rendered 'valuable service' at the Church of St Philip Neri.

'Only a year ago last August it may be remembered the Councillor and Mrs Glossop lost their other son, Sergeant WB Glossop of the Royal Garrison Artillery, aged 31, killed in action in France. Their eldest boy, William E Glossop of the Argyll and Sutherland Highlanders was killed in the Boer War at Paardeburg in March 1900.

At the monthly meeting of the Arundel Council on Thursday, a vote of sympathy was passed with Councillor WE Glossop in the death in action of his son. The Mayor said he hoped the sad hour would be brightened for the parents, by the knowledge of the fact that their son died fighting for his King and Country'.

======

Private William Francis KENT serving with the Royal Warwickshire Regiment was killed in action on 3 September 1917. He had previously enlisted at Horsham into the Royal Sussex Regiment. William had been born in New Fishbourne, Sussex, the son of Samuel, a gardener/domestic servant and his wife Maria. They had both originally lived in Chichester. William also became a gardener at New Fishbourne on leaving school before moving and working in Tortington, lodging at 65 Broad Green Cottages. It was not long after that William married Annie, the pair setting up home in Queen Street, Arundel, from where William enlisted.

======

In September 1917, the 12th Battalion, the Royal Sussex Regiment were heavily involved in the Menin Road area. On the morning of 25 September the Germans launched a heavy shelling attack along a wide front causing many casualties, Lance Sergeant George Arthur MILLS, aged 24 being one of them. George, who was the second son of bricklayer John and Matilda, had enlisted in Horsham. Previous to that he was employed as a Post Office Telegraph Messenger at Arundel.

======

'Deep sympathy will be felt for Mr and Mrs Maxwell-Stuart of Batworth Park whose second son Second Lieutenant Henry Joseph Ignatius MAXWELL-STUART, aged 30, is reported by the War Office to have been killed in action near Ypres on 9 October 1917. He is the third of their sons to have given their lives for their Country. He joined the 3rd Battalion, the Coldstream Guards about a year ago having previously served in the Rhodesian Rifles. When that Corps was temporarily disbanded he hastened home to enlist in England'.
Much sympathy was expressed for this well known family who received the news of the death of yet another son.

======

Trooper Charles Henry BERRYMAN, aged 21, the son of Charles, a wood sawyer and his wife Elizabeth, of Poling Street, was born in Arundel. On leaving school he was employed as a 'pottery boy'. He enlisted at Arundel into the Kent Yeomanry and at some stage transferred into the Household Cavalry. He was killed in action on 12 October; his parents receiving the news in a letter from his Squadron Sergeant Major;
'He went over the top with the Battalion on 12 October and was seen at a very advanced stage of the ground taken by us. When he was last seen he was fighting gallantly with his comrades and I cannot definitely say what become of him. It is quite probable that he may be a prisoner in Germany which I hope and trust may turn out to be true both for your sake and No 2

Company with whom he was very popular'.
This was a small hope, *'shared by the missing lads many friends in the village'.*

=====

The Arundel connection for Wilfred Scott is unknown. He was born near Salisbury, Wiltshire in 1896 where his father was the local blacksmith and enlisted in Salisbury into the Royal Garrison Artillery. Corporal Wilfred SCOTT was awarded the Military Medal and lost his life on 13 October, aged 19.

=====

1917 HOME FRONT

The bad news which swept Arundel at the beginning of 1917 was the death of a much loved Duke. The town was in mourning.
The school children were given a project to help them follow the progress of the war in which so many of their father's were fighting;
'Thanks to the Mayor, the school children have this spring learnt much that must be helpful to them in following the progress of the great work the nation is accomplishing. To compete for the handsome prizes he has offered they have had useful lessons on the war's work with special regard to the Western Front and to its geographical and technical aspects'.
During the war various Regiments made use of Arundel for training purposes;
'The Second Battalion, the Inns of Court, County of London Volunteer Regiment have spent Easter camping at Arundel. It was the fourth occasion they had visited and they developed their training in a thoroughly serious and practical manner being engaged in bayonet fighting, musketry drill and field operations. The Volunteers presented a very smart and soldierly appearance although about two hundred of their number couldn't make it because of war work'.
The food shortage was now of some concern and the growing of potatoes was actively encouraged, with plenty of advice on how to deal with diseases;
'Allotment holders on the Duke of Norfolk's Estate and others, not members of the Town Council, seem to have had some trouble in disposing of the haulms of diseased potatoes, but the Town Council have now permitted the use of the town tip for their disposal. The importance of preventing the disease from spreading was emphasised by the Mayor and to that end also growers were urged to destroy the little potatoes on diseased plants as they also retain the germ.
Under the direction of Privates H Maxwell-Stuart and F Jones, members of the local Volunteer Company who broke up a large plot of the Cricket Hill

Field and planted it with potatoes are now reaping a rich harvest. The seed was collected by the Volunteers and all freely contributed; the cultivation of the plot entailed much arduous work. The gratifying result, however, is keenly appreciated at the Red Cross Hospital where no shortage of "spuds" is anticipated.

And Boy Scouts, of the 1st Arundel Troop and the St Philips Troop have undertaken to support the National Egg Collection for the wounded. Sums of money, even of a penny or half penny would be gratefully accepted. It has been regretted that Arundel is the only place in the district, of which Chichester is the centre, where no such collection has been made for some months. Authorised collectors will wear a special badge'.

It was suggested that a war museum be organised, following the gift of a German helmet to the Council, from Dr Eustace, who was serving at the Front. The Victoria Institute was thought to be a suitable venue. Other objects which various Councillors were prepared to loan included an 18lb shell and a piece of a Zeppelin. Although the matter was referred to the General Purposes Committee and received the backing of the press, it seems to have progressed no further.

In November, following the death of his second son, Councillor W Glossop, accompanied by his wife and daughter, unveiled a 'handsome brass tablet' in memory of his two sons, which was fixed to the South Wall of St Philip Neri Church. The brief ceremony was attended by the Mayor of Arundel, Councillor Dorman and other members of the Council and many townsfolk.

The news from the war was bad. The 4th Battalion, the Royal Sussex Regiment, having withdrawn from Gallipoli were now involved in heavy fighting in Palestine and casualties were high;

'It is expected that the toll of casualties in the Palestine fighting would include some of our local lads as the 4th Battalion, the Royal Sussex were so heavily engaged there'

The prediction came true.

1918 WAR FRONT

'THE START OF THE VICTORY YEAR,
WE ARE ON THE ROAD TO VICTORY'

Were the headlines that greeted Arundel as 1918 dawned;

'It is difficult for readers who are not behind the scenes and acquainted with the game to realise the facts, the Great White Armies of Freedom are making ready to ram Germany this summer'.

The prophesy was to come true, but not before many more local men were wounded and twenty two were to lose their lives.

======

Able Seaman Jack DALTON was born and grew up in Arundel, one of seven children belonging to Thomas a carpenter/joiner and his wife Mercy. By 1901 the family lived in School Lane, but returned at some time to 93 Tarrant Street. Jack subsequently enlisted into the Royal Navy.

Jacks ship, HMS Raglan was built in 1914 one of a new class of monitors designed to carry eight fourteen inch guns for shore bombardment. The guns were originally built for a Greek battleship, being built by Germany, but the wartime British blockade cancelled this arrangement. The naming of the new ship caused a minor problem, planned to be called the Robert E Lee after the American soldier, the name was hastily changed to HMS Lord Raglan because of America's neutrality. Her name was changed again to HMS Raglan shortly before she sailed for the Dardenelles in June 1915. She spent all her time in the Mediterranean and on 20 January whilst devoid of her battleship escorts she was sunk by two Turkish battleships, the ex German SMS Goeben and SMS Breslau, with a loss of her one hundred and twenty seven crew. Able Seaman Jack Dalton was 30 years old.

======

Private Philip AYLING was born in Arundel where his father worked as a bricklayer. He was the fourth son of Mr and Mrs O Ayling, of 35 Bond Street.

On leaving school Philip became a grocer's errand boy before enlisting into the 14th Battalion, the Hampshire Regiment at Winchester. The 14th Battalion was formed in Portsmouth by the Mayor and a local committee before being adopted by the War Office in May 1915. After training in England, the Battalion arrived at Le Havre in July 1916 and were soon in action at Ancre and Thiepval.

In February 1917 Philip was wounded, being struck by fragments of a shell whilst having tea in a dugout. His foot being so injured as to require the amputation of a toe;

'I was lucky to get off'', he wrote to his mother, 'as my mate who was sitting next to me was killed'.

His luck ran out a year later when he received wounds from which he died.

The sad intimation has reached Mr and Mrs Owen Ayling, of that Private Philip John AYLING, aged 22, of the 14th Hants, one of their five soldier sons, has fallen in France. He died in a casualty clearing station hospital on 20 February from wounds received the previous day. He and his four brothers had all been previously wounded, the deceased about twelve months ago, when a severe wound in his foot necessitated the amputation of a toe. He returned to the fighting line only five weeks ago. Letters from the Roman Catholic Chaplain and a Sister from the hospital, couched in the most sympathetic terms, informed the bereaved parents of their loss and assured them that everything possible was done for him. He was laid to rest in a Roman Catholic Cemetery'.

=====

On 21 March the Germans launched a major offensive on the Western Front, to defeat the Allies before the United States, who had recently entered the war, could fully deploy its men and materials. Boosted by nearly five hundred thousand men transferred from their Russian Front, now that conflict had ended, the Germans made the deepest advances of either side during the four years of war, aimed at defeating the British and forcing the French to seek an Armistice. Many Allied soldiers were killed or wounded during the offensive which came to a halt towards the end of April, as the German supply lines failed to keep pace with the movement of their troops. They had also suffered heavy casualties.

=====

Eleven local soldiers lost their lives during the offensive, the first, Private Frederick K George HAMMOND, aged 34, being killed on the opening day.

The only son of Arundel born general builder and labourer John Hammond and his wife Emily, who came from South Stoke, Frederick was born and grew up in Arundel. He was still single, living at home and employed as a house painter and builder; according to the 1911 Census, the family were living at Arun Cottage, The Slipe. However, by the time of his death seven years later he had married Alice Alexandra from Cambridge and was serving in the Royal Army Service Corps after enlisting at Grove Park, London. He then transferred to the 8th Battalion, the Royal West Kent Regiment, which landed in France in August 1915. It was whilst serving with that Regiment, Frederick was killed in action.

=====

The following day Second Lieutenant Ernest ATTWATER was born in the mid Sussex village of Cuckfield, one of nine children of Alfred, who was a whitesmith and his wife, Frances. On leaving school he became a builder/carpenter, working with his brother, Frank, who was a builder/decorator. He married Alice Ethel Hull, an Arundel lass in 1917 making their home at 4 Fitzalan Terrace.

'Having enlisted he was serving in the 58th Battalion, the Machine Gun Corps becoming one of the fallen in the great struggle in France, age 29. His death has evoked much sympathy for his young widow, the daughter of Councillor and Mrs RW Hulls; there is a baby son by the marriage which took place about fourteen months ago. Lieutenant ATTWATER was formerly a member of the cricket staff at the Oval and saw much fighting in the earliest days of the war at Ypres, Loos and the Somme, where his meritorious work as a machine gunner earned for him the recognition of a Commission. The young Officer and his family are highly respected at their home in Cuckfield, where, as in Arundel, his loss will be deeply regretted'.

=====

Four days later Private Michael SMITH, the second son of William and Kate who had four other children, was killed in action; aged 19.The family lived at the Castle Stables where William was the groom. By the time he enlisted Michael had exchanged his life in Arundel and was living and working at Earls Court, London, where he enlisted at Sun Street into the 7th Battalion, the London Regiment. He was also killed in action during the Spring Offensive.

=====

Second Lieutenant Arthur Henry Edmund GUNNER, aged 28, had only been married five months when he was killed in action;
'At the Church of St Philip Neri in November 1917 the marriage was solemnized between Miss Emily May Watts, the eldest daughter of the late Mr AH Watts and of Mrs Watts of Meadowcroft, Station Road and Second Lieutenant Arthur Edmund Gunner, of the 3rd Battalion, the Royal Sussex Regiment, the eldest son of Mr and Mrs Gunner of Bank House, High Street'.
Arthur soon returned to duty and was killed in action on 27 March;
'Mr WH Gunner, the manager of the London County and Westminster Bank, of Bank House, Arundel, has heard that his eldest son, 2nd Lieutenant Arthur Edmund Gunner has been killed. The gallant young Officer, who was born in Arundel, was only married to Miss Watts, of Arundel recently. The sad bereavement follows so quickly on her happy marriage'.
In a letter of regret to his wife, Arthur's Commanding Officer, wrote;
'During my brief connection with him I found him to be a very popular and efficient Officer, who during heavy fighting behaved splendidly'.

=====

The next Arundel fatality occurred the following day;
'Mrs C Lynn, of Park Place, has received official notification that her eldest son, Private Charles Frank LYNN has been killed in France on 28 March. Only 19 years of age, Private Lynn was in the Irish Guards, enlisting at Whitehall in March 1917 and he went to France in November the same year'.
Born in Arundel, to Charles senior, a stonemason and Mary, Charles junior had a brother, Arthur and a sister, Mary. His father suffered from chronic rheumatism and had to give up work when Charles jnr. was still at school. Charles was formerly employed by Her Grace, the Duchess of Norfolk, both at the Castle and Norfolk House.

=====

Private George Stanley NASH was the youngest of three sons born to Thomas and Eliza, of River Road, and was a former Territorial who enlisted at Chichester into the 11th Battalion, the Royal Sussex Regiment. He was wounded on 21 March; the first day of the Offensive and according to the Sussex Roll of Honour was killed in action on 3 April. However, other Royal Sussex records give 21 March as his date of death, aged 19.

=====

Private Sydney Edward VICK was also from the Brighton area having been born there, where Sydney's father, Thomas, was the Receiving Officer for the local Board of Guardians; he subsequently transferred to Chichester, where Sydney worked as his assistant. Although his family continued to live in Chichester, Sydney enlisted into the 13th Battalion, the Royal Sussex Regiment and moved to Arundel prior to the war. Sydney was killed in action on 26 April, aged 27, during a mist camouflaged 'intense German machine gun attack'. He was one of twenty eight Royal Sussex Officers and men to lose their lives that day.

=====

Mr and Mrs Henry Taylor, of Bond Street, Arundel, lost two sons to the sea. The first was an unfortunate victim of the Titanic's doomed Atlantic crossing in 1912, the second was the loss of HMS Bombola and their third son Signaller Bruno Henry Edward TAYLOR on 2 May 1918. Bruno had not been home for five years and in his last letter to his parents he stated that he hoped to be seeing them shortly. His ship HMS Bombola, a converted collier, only equipped with two fourteen pounder guns, was involved in a hard fought surface action, lasting a couple of hours with two German submarines, U 153 and U 154, off the coast of Mauritania. It was an unequal fight and HMS Bombola was lost with all hands.

=====

Private Michael Phillip LEE lived at 12 Mount Pleasant, Arundel, with his parents and was employed as a grocer's assistant. He enlisted into the 1st Battalion, the Middlesex Regiment and died at home on 13 May, aged 27. The cause of death is unknown, however, there is a strong possibility he may have been a victim of the influenza pandemic.

=====

The 4th Battalion, the Royal Sussex Regiment having completed their Middle East duties were transferred to the Western Front. They left Alexandria on 17 June 1918 bound for Italy and then on to France, where after a long and weary journey, they arrived on 29 June. Here they undertook a certain amount of training including how to deal with gas attacks, something they had not previously encountered, as well as acclimatising to the wet, muddy conditions of Europe after many months in the hot, dry deserts. After a period in reserve they were sent to the Front and ordered to attack a wooded area near the Grand Rozoy on 29 July, which was taken after a bayonet charge. Some German machine guns were captured, not before they had accounted for two Arundel men.

=====

Private Arthur James BURCH, aged 27, was born in Arundel and on marrying Mildred lived with her parents at the Waterworks, Warningcamp, where his father in law worked. Recognised as a prominent footballer in

Arundel, Arthur was employed as a printer for the West Sussex Gazette, before enlisting. Serving with the 4th Sussex in Palestine he suffered a severe head wound in 1917 and was invalided home. Rejoining his Battalion in France he was also killed in the action of 29 July, aged 33, leaving his wife Mildred to bring up their young daughter, Ruth.

======

Thirteen months after the death of their son, Frederick, (see 1917) Mr James Swain, the Arundel Pearl Assurance Agent and his wife, Fanny, were notified that a second son, Private George SWAIN had been killed in the same action, aged 34. He had lived at 1 Gratwicke Terrace, South Marshes and was employed as a timber labourer before enlisting at Littlehampton into the 4th Battalion, the Royal Sussex Regiment.

======

The following month another son of Mr and the Hon. Mrs Maxwell-Stuart, of Batworth Park died of wounds on 24 August. He was their third son to lose his life in the war. Second Lieutenant Alfred Joseph MAXWELL-STUART was aged 20 and serving with the 1st Battalion the Coldstream Guards. He had recently been living in Dorset. Much sympathy was expressed to his parents on yet another loss and special prayers were said in Arundel Cathedral.

======

Private Alfred William CARVER was the son of Walter, a bricklayer and his wife Caroline and was born in Sutton, Sussex. The family moved to Arundel, living in Surrey Street, where Walter, now promoted to a Foreman Bricklayer working for the Duke of Norfolk's estate, with Alfred following his steps as an apprentice. Alfred was thirty one years old when war was declared and still single living with his parents at their new address, 15 Bond Street, Arundel. He enlisted at Chichester into the 7th Battalion, the Royal Sussex Regiment, probably in 1914 and served with them almost till the end of the conflict. In early September 1918 the 7th Battalion were attacking German positions approaching the village of Nurlu in the face of heavy machine gun fire, during which Alfred received wounds from which he died on 7 September, aged 35.

======

Private Ernest Victor LEWINGTON was born in London moving to Arundel with his wife, Helen and their two young children, where he worked as a bootmaker and repairer. He lived at St Juliana, Tarrant Street, Ernest enlisted in Horsham into the 7th Battalion, the Royal Sussex Regiment, who in September 1918 were resting for ten days having fought all through August in the renewed British offensive. On 18 September they were detailed to assemble near the village of Epehy, for what was described as a 'complicated manoeuvre' which depended solely on the village being taken early by other Regiments. The weather was bad, heavy rain giving way to thick mist, which added to the smoke caused by the

British artillery; this inevitably caused confusion and the loss of direction during the advance. Furthermore they encountered a barbed wire defence which had not been shown on the maps they were carrying. Having reached this they were subjected to heavy German machine gun fire from the village, which had not been taken as planned. The 7th Sussex lost many men there, including Private Ernest Lewington, aged 34.

======

Sergeant James HARWOOD MM lived at Orchard Place, Arundel, the son of Henry, a general labourer and Sarah. He was born in Arundel and on leaving school became a Post Office Messenger. He enlisted in Arundel, one of three brothers serving and the second one to be awarded the Military Medal. In December 1915 he was wounded in the Dardenelles and evacuated firstly to a Maltese hospital and then Shirley Hospital in Hampshire. He was wounded again in Palestine two years later.

'Mr and Mrs Harwood of Orchard Place, have received a letter from Lieutenant RB Mason, of the 4th Battalion, the Royal Sussex Regiment, stating that their son, was killed instantaneously, on 25 September, aged 22'.

James lost his life during an attack on the German held Spanbroekmolen Crater, being a member of several patrols 'who by stealth and determination drove out the enemy and occupied the crater'. They encountered heavy small arms fire, during which James was killed.

'How universally your son was liked and respected since he has been with the Battalion', wrote his Commanding Officer, 'as a non-commissioned Officer he has been quite invaluable and we knew he was always to be trusted in an emergency. We all feel we have lost a comrade whose place it will be impossible to fill'.

From the Chaplain the parents also received a letter of sympathy and tribute to their son, who had been previously wounded three times'

======

Like his father, Joseph Wills was born in Somerset, the family evidently moving to Arundel, the birthplace of his mother, Rhoda, at a later date. Joseph senior was employed as a stoker at the Gas Works, the family living in Park Place.

Joseph jnr was the eldest of six surviving children and had three brothers and two sisters. Originally enlisting at Arundel into the Royal Sussex Regiment, 1918 found him serving with the 1st Garrison Battalion of the Royal Norfolk Regiment in India where he died on October 29th 1918.

'An official intimation has reached Mrs J Wills, of South Marshes, that her husband, Private Joseph WILLS has succumbed to fever in hospital at Poona, India, age unknown. Private Wills joined Kitcheners Army in February 1915 and after training was sent to India, where he has been for nearly three years. Mrs Wills desires to thank all who have so kindly sympathised with her in her sad loss'.

Lance Corporal George ROBINSON was born in Arundel in 1886 and became one of if not the first motor omnibus driver in the town, driving the private bus operated by the Norfolk Hotel. At that time he and his wife Ellen lived at the Norfolk Tap. It was logical therefore that when he enlisted in Brighton his driving skills were utilised as a member of the Royal Army Service Motor Transport Corps.

'Particularly sad are the circumstances connected with the death of Lance Corporal George Robinson, aged 32, which took place at his home in Norfolk Tap last Saturday. He came home on leave from France about a fortnight previously, apparently in perfect health. After paying a visit to some relations in Norfolk, he returned to Arundel and fell victim to influenza, which was followed by double pneumonia. Much sympathy is felt for his widow and four young children'.

His wife, Ellen, received a most sympathetic letter from his Officer Commanding, referring to the death of her husband whilst home on leave;

'One of the steadiest men in the Company, he had the confidence of the Officers and Senior NCO's and was generally liked by all the men and the deepest sympathy of the entire Company goes out to you in your bereavement. During the recent operations, as no doubt he informed you himself, he had rather a rough time in advanced positions and this evidently affected his health, for on his return to the Company, prior to going on leave, many remarked upon his altered appearance'.

=====

Stoker 1st Class George HAMMOND, the son of James, a labourer and Ada, was born in Arundel and lived his early life in Poling, Sussex. George joined the Royal Navy serving on HMS Redoubtable, when he was taken ill and placed in the Royal Naval hospital at Hasler, Portsmouth. He passed away, possibly from pneumonia aged 24.

=====

Another probable victim of the Influenza Pandemic was Private Herbert STEWART aged 28, the son of George and Elizabeth Stewart, who was born in Arundel, where his father was a foreman on the Duke of Norfolk's Estate. On leaving school Herbert worked as a groom at Park Farm before enlisting in Chichester into the Royal Sussex Regiment. He later joined the Labour Corps, which consisted largely of those who were not considered to be in A1 condition for Front line fighting, although very often they worked within the range of the enemy guns and during the March Retreat of 1918 were used as emergency infantry. At the time of his death at home his address was given as the **Castle Dairy** where he lived with his wife Emily.

=====

The son of painter Allan and his wife, Eliza, Private Bertram BLACKMAN was born in Maltravers Street, Arundel. The family moved to Park Place, but Bertram was soon on the move, living in Portslade, East

Sussex, where he worked as a house painter. At some stage in the years prior to the war he took the decision to emigrate to Canada. Bertram enlisted into the Canadian Pioneers, formed in 1916 as part of the Canadian Division and returned to England, leaving his wife and three children at home. He subsequently became a victim of the Influenza Pandemic and died on 25 October and was buried in Brighton. He was given a military funeral locally, his coffin being bourne to his grave by six members of the Royal Army Medical Corps, who also provided a firing party with buglers sounding the Last Post.

=====

The last Arundel man to lose his life, just three days before the Armistice, was Private Richard BUTCHER aged 42, the son of David, a groom and his wife, Charlotte. Richard was born in Arundel, the family living in the town, firstly in Queen Street and then River Road. Giving up his job as a brewer's labourer he originally enlisted in 1897 into the Army Service Corps fighting in the South African Wars, receiving both the Queen's and King's Medals. He had served in the Great War since August 1914 re-enlisting into the 12th Battalion, the Kings Royal Regiment. Well known and a popular figure in Arundel, he was gassed followed by influenza and passed away on 8 November; a sad end for a soldier who almost saw the war through to completion.

=====

Stoker First Class K34462 James FLYNN was the son of the verger of St Philip Neri. Little is known of him. He served in the Royal Navy on HMS Invincible, before joining HMS Dianthus, a newly built Escort Sloop. They were deliberately designed to resemble merchant men, with weapons hidden away out of sight. Whilst HMS Dianthus served the last days of the war off the West African coast James Flynn died. The details of his death on 23 November 1918 have not come to light, be it accidental or illness.

1918 HOME FRONT

In Arundel food shortages were becoming critical and a Food Control Committee was set up;
'Our town had its first experience of queues on Saturday. The three butcher's shops, which by arrangement with the Food Control Committee, opened at nine o'clock, were besieged and under the watchful eyes of the members of that authority meat was distributed. Although there was a division among the traders of eleven deer from the park, the meat available was not sufficient to go round and tears were not altogether absent from unsuccessful housewives.'
A few days later at a meeting at the Castle, the Duchess of Norfolk revealed that an effort was to be made to establish a public kitchen in the

town, where;

'Children could get most nourishing penny dinners and people could obtain or take away meals at less cost than they could prepare them individually at home'.

A week or two later an 'instructive address' was given at the Town Hall, by a Mrs Green, of the Economy Section of the Ministry of Food, who at the invitation from and at the expense of, the Duchess, spoke about food economy and the advantages of a national kitchen in Arundel, which already had the support of local housewives and the Town Council. Suitable premises had been found and the scheme now only awaited the sanction of the Ministry of Food.

The scheme, however, never got off the ground, the premises the Council had in view, 'which had been vacant for a considerable period' had suddenly been let for three months and the authorities had not yet sanctioned the formation of a food kitchen, because 'Arundel was too small'. The Council still keen to go ahead then deferred the matter until the autumn, but events overtook it and the scheme was dropped.

Meanwhile, the Food Control Committee had introduced food rationing and Ration Books were issued;

'Which on the whole caused few complaints, but it would seem that butchers or their assistants have not yet quite mastered the mathematical niceties involved!'

Apart from meat, the price of milk and sugar also came under their control. Milk prices for the summer months were fixed at 1s 8d (8p) a gallon, soon to rise to 2s (10p) a gallon and permits for the purchase of sugar for jam making were issued from 8 June;

'In view of the fact that the recent spell of fine weather is likely to result in the early ripening of fruit crops, it has been decided by the Arundel Food Control Committee that in any case where the special supplies of sugar that are being issued, have not been received by a retailer and where the withholding of supplies would result in the fruit being wasted, he may honour these permits out of his ordinary stocks, so far as these are available and a General Licence to this effect is now being issued. This privilege should, however, be used only by those permit holders who are in immediate need of sugar in order to avoid loss of fruit'.

Instructions were published for the collection of blackberries for jam making, with the Food Control Committee appointing a local Executive Officer to oversee the same. Pickers were given clear instructions;

'Fruit must be picked free from stem and should be picked dry and should remain fit for jam making for two to four days after picking'.

Pickers were paid 3d (2p) per pound, when the fruit was taken to the Local Food Office inspected and weighed. Local schoolchildren attacked this task with a passion, collecting four hundredweight of blackberries. In all over eleven hundredweights were collected and despatched within a few days, along with nearly the same weight in marrows from the Arundel allotment holders. They had benefitted from a talk by Mr FC Legge, the head gardener to the Duke of Norfolk's estate entitled 'Practical Hints on Gardening', concentrating on the growing of potatoes and other vegetables. He also emphasised the importance of growing beans and sugar beet, in which he had already made a successful experiment.

The Arundel and District Cottage Hospital opened in the early spring;

'An absolute necessity, particularly in times like the present, when the presence of a hospital close at hand might be the means of saving life'.

The hospital was opened by the Duchess of Norfolk accompanied by her two young children in the presence of a large number of dignitaries and townspeople, including a guard of honour provided by the newly formed Arundel Girl Guides. The maintenance of the hospital was undertaken by the townspeople, many of whom had voluntarily promised a small weekly sum towards its upkeep.

=====

PEACE RETURNS

The signing of the Armistice on 11 November saw Arundel en fete;

'Immediately upon receipt of the glad news of the signed Armistice, on Monday, the inhabitants, almost without exception, displayed flags from houses and shops. The Union Jack was hoisted on the historic Castle, the Town Hall and the Churches. Strings of bunting were stretched across the main streets, British emblems being interspersed with the Tri-Colour and other flags of the Allies.

Soon sounds of the bugle resounded as the Boy Scouts marched through the town and many children also formed themselves into processions having improvised bands with the aid of tin boxes and sang Rule Britannia as they gaily marched along waving flags.

As the evening wore on the inhabitants crowded into the centre of town and there was much cheering, alternating with sounds of bugle and drum, together with much more music from the "band". Rockets, too, were sent up and the youngsters had much fun with crackers, when the kindly policeman looked the other way!'

WOUNDED SOLDIERS AND CHILDREN OUTSIDE THE WEST SUSSEX GAZETTE OFFICE WHICH WAS DISPLAYING A COPY OF THE ARMISTICE TELEGRAM

Further celebrations concentrating on the wounded soldiers took place at the Red Cross Hospital.

'When the announcement of the signing of the Armistice was displayed the wounded soldiers at the Red Cross Hospital were amongst the most jubilant of demonstrators. On Thursday evening Her Grace, the Duchess of Norfolk, recognising the part that these gallant fellows had played in bringing about such a glorious result, entertained the soldiers, nurses and helpers at the hospital to a dance to celebrate the cessation of hostilities. Her Grace, accompanied by the young Duke and Lady Rachel, with guests from the Castle, attended the dance, which had just commenced when they entered the gaily decorated ward. The Duchess who wore her Red Cross uniform mounted the platform and after each one present had been handed champagne, she called for the company to drink the health of the King. Her Grace referred to the signing of the Armistice as one of the greatest events in the history of the Country and in graceful phrases she thanked the soldiers for what they had done for us.

The Duchess then joined in the "Lancers", with one of the wounded for a partner, the Duke dancing with one of the nurses, after which the Castle party left. Dancing was kept up until about 11 30pm there being an interval for supper. At the close cheers were given for all who had contributed to the success of a memorable and joyous evening, especially for Sister Wood, who, with the Quartermaster, Mrs GS Constable, had done so much for the comfort of the company. The music was provided by

Mr and Mrs RG Blackman'.
(Mr Blackman was a Professor of Music, who lived in Tarrant Street).
======

Thoughts soon turned to the return of the boys;
'To the Mayor would fall the honour of welcoming home many men of the town who had been fighting for King and Country. No less than 22.7 per cent of Arundel's manhood had served in Her Majesty's Forces, a record of which they were all justly proud. Some of them would not return; they had given their lives for freedom and their memory would remain forever green in the ancient Borough'.

Gradually the men arrived back home, but not all. The 4th Battalion, the Royal Sussex Regiment, (Territorial's) were kept in France, spending another Christmas away from home. They had had a tough war, having been away since the Gallipoli campaign of 1915, before moving to Egypt and Palestine. Then a quick move to the Western Front in 1918, having to re-acclimatise from the hot arid deserts, to the wet and muddy European conditions, they played a significant part in the final days of the war. Led by both Mrs Campion, the wife of Colonel Campion, 4th Sussex and Mrs Guy Constable, the wife of Major Constable a considerable amount of Christmas fare and presents were collected from the towns folk and sent to the men, "a laudable effort", commented the paper.

During 1919 the rest of the Arundel heroes returned.

Celebrations focused on the 'Boys', when over three hundred Arundel sailors, soldiers and airmen, discharged and demobilised, were entertained to a dinner and concert paid for by the subscriptions of the towns inhabitants;
'Accompanied by a band composed of ex 4th Battalion, Royal Sussex Bandsmen and the band of the Royal Sussex 2nd Battalion, the men, amid cheering crowds, marched through the be-flagged town, from New Road by way of Tarrant Street, Maltravers Street and London Road to the Castle Grounds. On the walls of the St Mary's Gate were fixed two large boards, on which in letters and figures, in red, white and blue, were recorded the words;
"Peace with Victory, thanks to the Boys, Arundel is proud of you".
Inside the Castle the route was lined by smart Girl Guides and Boy Scouts'.

After an excellent meal, Lord Edmund Talbot, the Arundel MP, proposing the toast to the Fallen, remarked that even on such an occasion of rejoicing they should be mindful of those who gave their lives in the Great War. He then referred to the missing;
'You know there is an anxious feeling amongst some people that some of the missing may yet be found. I am sorry but I must destroy any such hope. We (the Government) are now absolutely convinced from all the inquiries we have made, there is no single case of a missing man where there is any

hope of life. I say that and I repeat it, I know there are many still thinking and hoping that out of the great mass of the missing, their loved ones may return and it is only right that they should be told, sorrowful and miserable though it is, that there is no hope whatsoever'.

THE VICTORY BOARDS AND MINE HOSTS OUTSIDE THE ST MARY'S GATE

He then asked the men to stand for a few moments to remember their fallen comrades, 'many were deeply affected; it was an unforgettable moment'

=====

The signing of the peace treaty with Germany at 4pm on 28 June 1919 was received with much celebration in Arundel;

'When shortly after four o'clock the news of the signing of the Peace Treaty was received, the Union Flag was hoisted on the Castle and the flags of the Allies speedily appeared from many windows on private houses and business premises, being in several instances suspended across the main thoroughfares.

Services at the Parish Church and St Philip Neri attracted crowded congregations, who heartily joined in the singing of the National Anthem and the Te Deum.

A dance, organised by the Women's Guild of the Arundel Co-operative Society, was held at the Town Hall, the Mayor, to mark the great event of the day, sanctioning its continuance to midnight. From numbers and spirit it was pronounced a success. American soldiers were there'.

Saturday, 19 July, was the day of national celebration of victory and peace. The Government declared a Bank Holiday and throughout the country, towns and villages arranged their own peace programmes. At Arundel the festivities commenced on the preceding Wednesday, when His Grace, the Duke of Norfolk, entertained the current and retired workers from both his Sussex and Surrey estates, at the Castle, plus the returned estate soldiers with their wives and children, where they were entertained to a 'bounteous dinner'.

(During the dinner reference was made to the fact that one hundred years earlier a similar function was held at the Castle, following the victory at Waterloo).

Dinner music was provided by the Band of the Royal Marine Artillery. In his speech, the Duke expressed his great pleasure to welcome home those who had so loyally served and hoped that they would never have to face such an ordeal like that again.

The following day the Duchess invited 'every man, woman and child' in Arundel to an 'At Home Day' at the Castle.

'To the beautiful park they wended their way from all directions to the High Street entrance of the Castle, as the clock in the Square struck four and through the lovely glades, ascended the bank leading to the extensive lawn, where they were received by the Duchess. Tea was served in two large marquees by the staff from a London catering firm. There were delicious cakes and ices, served unsparingly and how the children's eyes beamed at those pink ices and with what glee they swallowed them'.

The event continued with clowns, Punch and Judy, sports and catching the greasy pig, which caused chaos in the marquees where the animal ran to avoid being caught. A fireworks display centred on the Hiorne Tower bought the day to an end;

'The large and powerful fireworks created a fairyland scene in national colours, a grand salvo of rockets emitting myriads of multi coloured stars'.

The display lasted an hour and ended with the words 'Victory', 'Peace' and 'Thanks to the Boys', followed by a colossal fire portrait of the King.

Amid these events came the news that the Duke had made a gift of £500 to the Town 'in celebration of the Armistice, to be allocated to existing organisations in the town'. It was left to the Town Council to decide who would benefit.

======

The Belgium people now liberated from the German occupation were still in need of help. In response to an appeal by the National Committee for Relief in Belgium, the Arundel Committee were able to send over six hundred new and used garments plus money collected in Burpham, Poling and Tortington Churches.

This was one of the last actions of the Arundel voluntary war workers organisations, who were publicly thanked by the Duchess of Norfolk at a ceremony at the Castle, when 'numerous War Badges' were issued to the Red Cross Hospital staff. Opened in 1915, subsequently becoming an auxiliary to Graylingwell, the hospital closed soon after the Armistice was signed, having nursed five hundred and thirty patients in three and a half years. The Arundel Red Cross, many of whose members had devoted over fifteen hundred hours of duty each, were recognised for their support of the hospital, both in nursing and cooking the patients meals each day. As were the men's VAD, whose forty one members, unable to perform military service, helped every evening as orderlies at the hospital, bathing patients and completing many other tasks.

Other badge recipients included residents who regularly supplied eggs and potatoes, raised money, contributed to the cigarette fund, the Arundel Girl Guides Pierrot Troop and Mr Blackman, who entertained the patients. Special mention was made of Sister Wood, 'for the way she worked for the men, getting up whist drives every week, making cakes and many other things which helped towards their comfort'.

Voluntary Workers Badges were presented to the members of the local War Work Depot and its helpers from, Burpham, Lyminster, Poling, Warningcamp and Yapton. During the conflict they had made and sent away nearly nineteen thousand articles of clothing, including mittens, socks, sunshields and mufflers, as well as almost four thousand bandages.

=====

THE ARUNDEL BRITISH LEGION

The welfare of the ex servicemen was high on the national agenda and four organisations were formed, the Comrades of the Great War, the National Federation of Discharged and Demobilised Sailors and Soldiers, the National Association of Discharged Sailors and Soldiers and the Officers Association, to represent their interests. All these organisations were anxious to set up a branch in Arundel, the choice, however, was put to the ex servicemen at a meeting held in the Town Hall in April 1919, chaired by the then Mayor, Alderman Bartlett.

Feelings were running high amongst some of the servicemen at the meeting over injustices to men throughout the country in the way some had been treated;

The man that has been wounded or the widow who has lost the breadwinner are entitled to the same protection by the State as the employee who meets with an accident gets under the Employers Liability Act', stated one ex sailor.

'What about the employer, who having undertaken to re-instate his employee on his return from the war, did not carry out his promise', voiced another.

One irksome issue were the wartime Tribunals which exempted some from fighting;

'The soldier, now he was home would want to know how it was that he had to go and fight while the Tribunals ruled his neighbour did not have to'.

Other issues raised included the part women had played in the war, filling up the places of men and whether now the men had returned was it not the time for them to give up and allow the men their jobs back? And it was agreed that no-one wanted to see the return of the days following the Crimean and Boer Wars, when ex soldiers were standing at street corners, with cap in hand, receiving charity.

Clearly the case for joining one of these organisations was proved, but which one? The meeting was asked to decide; in a closely fought contest, the Federation of Discharged Sailors and Soldiers won by just four votes.

The Arundel Branch held its inaugural meeting at the Red Lion, before moving to a 'new and commodious club room 'at the Abercrombie Inn. Within a few weeks its membership had topped the hundred mark, a small balance was in the bank and a Benevolent Fund was started using the £100, being their share of the Dukes Armistice gift to the town.

In 1921 the British Legion was formed nationally, thus replacing the existing ex servicemen's organisations. Now all ex-servicemen had one voice to look after their welfare. The Arundel Branch replaced the active local branch of the National Federation and included ex servicemen from the outlying villages. The local Federation had already formed a band which was soon transformed into the Arundel British Legion Band, which became a popular attraction at local events.

=====

ARUNDEL'S WAR MEMORIALS

There are two War Memorials in Arundel. The first to be dedicated was a Memorial Tablet, subscribed for by the congregation of St Philip Neri, bearing the names of the men of the Catholic faith who died in the war, 'during a service of moving beauty and impressiveness'. When the Tablet was unveiled by the young Duke of Norfolk on a Sunday evening in June 1921, 'it seemed that almost all the people of Arundel, headed by the robed Mayor and Corporation were present'.

The Tablet was dedicated by Bishop Keating's, the Chaplain-General to the Roman Catholic Forces, followed by the Last Post; 'the service was one predominantly of music and all who heard it will long remember the truly wonderful singing of the choir'

Councillor W Glossop had a personal 'handsome Brass Tablet' fixed to the South Wall of St Philip Neri, in memory of his two sons Sergeant Wilfred Glossop of the Royal Garrison Artillery who died of wounds in 1916 and Corporal Walter Glossop of the Royal Sussex Regiment who was killed in action in 1917. This ceremony was attended by the Mayor of Arundel,

Councillor Dorman and other Councillors; Canon MacCall officiated.

In March 1920, the then Mayor of Arundel, Major GS Constable, MC, announced that he would shortly be putting before the townspeople the design for a Market Cross and drinking fountain, to be erected in the Town Square, as a public memorial to the Arundel men who fell during the war. Included in the Memorial would be the names of the late Duke of Norfolk, who was a Colonel of the 4th Battalion, the Royal Sussex Regiment, as well as being 'a great friend and benefactor to the town' and the late Colonel EJ Mostyn, their former Commanding Officer, whose ill health had forced him to step down on the eve of the Battalion going to war. He passed away shortly afterwards. It was further stated that before his death the late Duke had often expressed the wish that a Market Cross would be chosen as the town's War Memorial and the proposed scheme met with the full approval of the Duchess of Norfolk. Subsequently Major CR Godman (4th Royal Sussex Regiment) was asked to submit a design which would be presented to the townsfolk at a public meeting in due course. The was held in the Town Hall one Monday evening in April, when it was decided to erect a Memorial Cross in the Town Square, but at the same time to appoint a committee to consider other designs and report back at a further meeting.

The final design Major Godman presented took the form of a tapering shaft, surmounted by a Celtic Cross, complete with a water trough, which would cost an estimated £1,100. Her Grace, the Duchess had promised a 'generous donation' of £500, to which was added further pledges of £300 from individuals, leaving a shortfall of some £300. It was then decided to dispense with the water trough, 'in these days of motor traffic', which saved £200, leaving a sum approaching £100 for 'the inhabitants to subscribe'. The design was then approved, with the amendment that the provision of a ledge at the base would be removed as it would be used as a seat, 'perhaps by youthful lady-killers smoking cigarettes', which would thus desecrate the purpose of the Memorial.

LORD LECONFIELD HAVING UNVEILED THE WAR MEMORIAL

At noon on Sunday 21 July 1921, Arundel's War Memorial was unveiled; *'Burgesses of Arundel, of distinguished or humble origin, young or old, healthy or infirm, gathered in the Square on Sunday afternoon, united by a common bond of sympathy. The town's War Memorial was to be unveiled and they stood in the full noon day heat, till the Square and the pavement halfway up Castle Hill were thronged. Police from many parts of the Division ably controlled the crowds and passage for traffic. Formed up in the Square were the Arundel members of the British Legion, under Major GS Constable MC. Both troops of scouts paraded, under their respective Scoutmasters and the Arundel detachment of the V.A.D. nurses were in attendance, under the Commandant, Her Grace the Duchess of Norfolk.*
The base of the Memorial was covered by the Union Jack, behind which in black lettering were listed the names of the ninety three fallen, those names to which the band of bereaved relatives at the foot of the monument meant more than the mere passing of some brave warriors'.
The Mayor, Councillor EJ Herington, the Town Clerk, Mr A Holmes and the Aldermen and members of the Town Council arrived in their civic robes. Earl Leconfield, the Lord Lieutenant of the County, arrived in military uniform and was attended to by His Grace, the Duke of Norfolk.

ARUNDEL WAR MEMORIAL UNVEILED BY LORD LECONFIELD, JULY 24, 1921

ARUNDEL MOURNS

The Mayor then read out the names of the fallen after which Lord Leconfield mounted the steps and pulled aside the flag which veiled them. He addressed the assembly, saying 'how proud he was to be invited to unveil the War Memorial', he continued;

'This Memorial is made of stone in order that it may commemorate for all time the names of those who went from this town and died in the most sacred of causes, in doing their duty for King and Country. All residents will thus be constantly reminded of those who paid the supreme sacrifice and I hope it will remind the future generation of duty nobly done. Those who have seen the devastated regions of France and Belgium know what sort of state this Country would now be in if these brave men had not gone forth and fought for their land. It would be most magnificent if war could be done away with, but in my opinion the change in human nature would have to be so great I am afraid it will never come to pass. Certainly until that was accomplished, it was our bounden duty to keep ourselves fit and ready to fight for our homes and Country. I hope this town will be inspired by the glorious faith of the men who died'.

The War Memorial was then dedicated by the Vicar of Arundel and prayers were read. At the conclusion, two buglers from the old 4th Battalion, the Royal Sussex Regiment, sounded the Last Post and Reveille, followed by the National Anthem, played by the Arundel Band of the British Legion and soon after the base of the War Memorial was hidden beneath 'a wealth of flowers'

PART TWO
THE ARUNDEL ROLL CALL

Listed below are the names of those who left Arundel to fight during the four year conflict; great care and time were spent in researching these and I trust the list is complete.

ADAMS, A - SIGNALLER
ROYAL FUSILIERS

ADAMS, THOMAS RICHARD, - PRIVATE
ROYAL CANADIAN HIGHLANDERS
South Marshes, Arundel

AID, WHF
MERCANTILE MARINE
Arundel

ALCORN, GEORGE FREDERICK PERKINS
AUSTRALIAN MOUNTED DIVISION
Tarrant Street, Arundel

ALSFORD, RONALD WILLIAM – PRIVATE
ARMY SERVICE CORPS
9 Wood View, Arundel

ANDREWS, G - PRIVATE
4th ROYAL SUSSEX REGIMENT
Arundel

ANGWIN, JAMES THIBOU - CAPTAIN
ROYAL FIELD ARTILLERY

Maltravers Street, Arundel

'Many residents serving in the Army have recently been seen and welcomed in our streets. Among them is Lieutenant Angwin, a Veterinary Officer on sick leave, fresh from the scenes of the new offensives now being pushed against the Germans in the West' (August 1918),

ARBERY, CHARLES EDWARD - LANCE CORPORAL
9th BATTALION THE CHESHIRE REGIMENT
Eagle Inn, Tarrant Street

ARBERY, GEORGE - SIGNALLER
ROYAL FUSILIERS
Eagle Inn, Tarrant Street

ARCHIBALD, CL - SERGEANT
ROYAL FLYING CORPS

ATKINS, GEORGE MONTAGUE - AIRMAN
ROYAL AIR FORCE
Cycle Agent, Tarrant Street

ATKINS, THOMAS LESLIE - AIRMAN
ROYAL AIR FORCE
Cycle Agent, Tarrant Street

ARTLETT, WA - GUNNER
GUNNERY SCHOOL, PORTSMOUTH

ATTWATER, ERNEST - PRIVATE
MACHINE GUN CORPS
KILLED IN ACTION 1918

ALSFORD, RONALD WILLIAM - PRIVATE
ROYAL ARMY SERVICE CORPS
9 Wood View, Ford Road, Arundel

AYLING, A - PRIVATE
2nd HAMPSHIRE REGIMENT

AYLING, ALBERT - PRIVATE
4th ROYAL SUSSEX REGIMENT
Arundel

AYLING, BENJAMIN G - LANCE CORPORAL
4th ROYAL SUSSEX REGIMENT
Wood View, Ford Road, Arundel
KILLED IN ACTION 1917

AYLING, ARCHIBALD BERNARD PHILIP - LANCE CORPORAL
4th ROYAL SUSSEX REGIMENT
1 Rose Terrace, Kirdford Road, Arundel

AYLING, CHARLES BERNARD - CORPORAL
4th ROYAL SUSSEX REGIMENT
2 Rose Terrace, Kirdford Road, Arundel
In August 1917 two brothers, Charles Ayling of the Royal Sussex
Regiment and Herbert Ayling of the Hampshire Regiment, sons of Mr and
Mrs Ayling of Offham have met in Palestine having been separated for five
years. Herbert had been following on the heels of his brother during the
war but had never succeeded in finding him until recently when he heard of
the presence of his Regiment in the district and obtained leave to meet him.
To his mother he writes;
"I had a job to recognise him, he would have passed me had I not hit him
on the shoulder and didn't he look surprised. He was just going to have a
wash but of course when he saw me it was a wash out".

AYLING, EDWARD GEORGE - PRIVATE
MACHINE GUN CORPS
35 Bond Street, Arundel

AYLING, HERBERT - PRIVATE
HAMPSHIRE REGIMENT

AYLING JJ - PRIVATE
2nd ROYAL SUSSEX REGIMENT
35 Bond Street, Arundel

In September 1914 Private JJ Ayling serving with the 2nd Battalion the Royal Sussex Regiment was wounded by shrapnel embedded in his jaw whilst fighting in the Battle of the Marne and was sent back at the Chichester Depot. In December he was discharged from hospital and went to Ireland to join his wife.

AYLING, JO - SERGEANT
2nd HAMPSHIRE REGIMENT
35 Bond Street, Arundel

Sergeant Ayling was serving in India in 1914 before taking part in the Gallipoli Campaign. He was 'wounded by a bullet in the right shoulder on 2 May whilst serving with the British Expeditionary Force in the Dardenelles. He is in the Egyptian Government Hospital at Port Said and is to be X-rayed to locate the bullet'. Sergeant Ayling was then transferred to hospital in Liverpool.

'Mr and Mrs Owen Ayling of Bond Street have received Official Notification that Sergeant JO Ayling of the 2nd Hampshire Regiment is suffering from severe gunshot wounds to the right arm and left foot. He is now in hospital in Liverpool. Sergeant Ayling was also wounded in Gallipolli' (May 1917).

He was the brother of Private JJ Ayling and Private WA Ayling

AYLING, OLIVER GEORGE - PRIVATE
LABOUR CORPS
6 Rose Terrace, Kirdford Road, Arundel

AYLING, PJ - PRIVATE
15TH HAMPSHIRE REGIMENT
35 Bond Street, Arundel
DIED OF WOUNDS 1918

AYLING, SIDNEY CHARLES - PRIVATE
ROYAL ENGINEERS
Tarrant Street, Arundel

AYLING, WILLIAM AUGUSTINE - PRIVATE
MACHINE GUN CORPS

35 Bond Street, Arundel
Private Ayling was wounded in January 1917 by a shell in the right thigh;
"he is going on well" writes the Chaplain "and in less pain."

AYLING, WILLIAM HAROLD - SIGNALLER
ROYAL ENGINEERS
Tarrant Street, Arundel

AYLING, W J - PRIVATE
4 BATTALION ROYAL SUSSEX REGIMENT
87 Surrey Street, Arundel
KILLED IN ACTION 1917

AYLWARD, PERCY - PRIVATE
1st SCOTS GUARDS REGIMENT
Arundel
KILLED IN ACTION 1914

BACKLOG T
1st NEW SOUTH WALES INFANTRY BRIGADE
AUSTRALIAN FORCES
Arundel
EMIGRATED AND RETURNED TO FIGHT

BAILEY, H - PRIVATE
SOUTH STAFFORDSHIRE REGIMENT

BAKER, EDWARD - GUNNER
ROYAL HORSE ARTILLERY
24 South Marshes, Arundel

BAKER, EDWARD PERCIVAL JOHN - LANCE CORPORAL
4th ROYAL SUSSEX REGIMENT
Mill Road, Arundel

BAKER, EDWIN FRANCIS - PRIVATE
QUEENS ROYAL WEST SURREY REGIMENT
King Street, Arundel

BAKER, GEORGE HENRY WILLIAM - SERGEANT
45th COMPANY ARMY SERVICE CORPS
12 Mount Pleasant, Arundel

BALCHIN, ALAN LESLIE - PRIVATE
ROYAL SUSSEX REGIMENT
Tarrant Street, Arundel

BALCHIN, ARTHUR EDWARD - PRIVATE
7th ROYAL SUSSEX REGIMENT
Tarrant Street, Arundel

BALCHIN, CHARLES DOUGLAS - PRIVATE
9th ROYAL SUSSEX REGIMENT
Tarrant Street, Arundel

BALCHIN, LA - PRIVATE
2nd ROYAL SUSSEX REGIMENT
Tarrant Street, Arundel

Writing to a friend in Arundel in May 1915, Private LA Balchin described his part in the ill- fated one day Battle of Aubers Ridge, which cost the lives of nearly three hundred men of the 2nd Battalion, the Royal Sussex Regiment: 'many brave men were mowed down, the ground within fifty yards of the start line was quickly littered with the dead and wounded,' wrote one report. Private Balchin wrote:

'The 2nd Royal Sussex Regiment went into action last Sunday. We lost heavily, but I came through without a scratch. The bombardment started about five o'clock in the morning and we charged at half past five. We had only got three parts of the way from our trench to the German trench and had to dig ourselves in. Then the word came to get back as best we could. As luck would have it there was a ditch running into our trench alongside of me, so I managed to get into this and crawl back. I was wet through up to my waist, but safe'.

BALCHIN, WH - SERGEANT
QUEENS OWN CANADIAN RIFLES
CANADIAN FORCES
Bakers Hill, Arundel
In 1915 news was received that Corporal W H Balchin had been wounded in the head and shoulder by a high explosive shell in France on 15 June. He is the second son of Mr G Balchin of Bakers Hill and has three brothers in the Army. He is now in hospital at Much Wenlock, Shropshire'.
WOUNDED IN JUNE 1915

BANKS, WJ - LIEUTENANT
Arundel
In April 1918 Lieutenant Banks was 'amongst the names of Officers recommended to the Secretary of State for War 'for valuable services rendered in connection with the war'.

BARKSHIRE, CR - CAPTAIN
ROYAL ENGINEERS
Arundel

BARKSHIRE, F - SERGEANT
VICTORIAN FUSILIERS
CANADIAN FORCES
Tarrant Street, Arundel
EMIGRATED AND RETURNED TO FIGHT

BARRETT, HENRY JOSEPH JNR. - LANCE CORPORAL
EAST KENT REGIMENT
River Road, Arundel
In October 1915 Mrs H Barrett of River Road heard through the War Office that her son Private H J Barrett was in hospital in Malta suffering from Pyrexia. Two years later, now a Lance Corporal he was invalided back to England in Southend Hospital, suffering from a gunshot wound to his left thigh'.
On returning to Egypt in June 1917 he suffered from dysentery, but was reported as 'doing well'.

BARRETT, HENRY SNR. - PRIVATE
24th BATTALION THE RIFLE BRIGADE

River Road, Arundel

BARRETT, MR - LANCE CORPORAL
1st BATTALION ROYAL SUSSEX REGIMENT
River Road, Arundel
The husband of Mrs Barrett of River Road, Arundel and a regular soldier,
who was stationed in India; Mr and Mrs Barrett had two sons serving plus
four brothers and two brothers in laws 'doing their bit'.

BARRETT, ROBERT FREDERICK GEORGE - PRIVATE
ROYAL SUSSEX REGIMENT
River Road, Arundel

BARTLETT, DOUGLAS - LIEUTENANT
ROYAL GARRISON ARTILLERY
High Street, Arundel

BARTLETT, D - LANCE CORPORAL
ROYAL ARMY MEDICAL CORPS

BARTLETT, WILLIAM EDWARD - PRIVATE
FORESTRY COMPANY, ROYAL ENGINEERS
Maltravers Street, Arundel

BEADLE, B - PRIVATE
4th ROYAL SUSSEX REGIMENT
Arundel
Wounded 1916

BEAMES, THOMAS W
HMS VINDICTIVE, ROYAL NAVY

BENHAM, PERCY JAMES - GUNNER
ROYAL FIELD ARTILLERY
Maltravers Street, Arundel

BENNETT, ARCHIBALD JAMES - PRIVATE
1st BATTALION ROYAL SUSSEX REGIMENT
2 Norfolk Terrace, Arundel

BENNETT, EJ - PRIVATE
4th BATTALION ROYAL SUSSEX REGIMENT
2 Norfolk Terrace, Arundel

BENNETT, REGINALD CHARLES – PRIVATE
1st BATTALION ROYAL SUSSEX REGIMENT
2 Norfolk Terrace, Arundel

BENTLEY, HUBERT HARRY- AIRMAN
ROYAL AIR FORCE
Mount Pleasant, Arundel

BERNARD, EDWARD VINCENT - PRIVATE
AGRICUTURAL CORPS
20 Bond Street, Arundel

BERRY, ARTHUR HENRY - PRIVATE
LABOUR CORPS
134 Park Farm Cottages

BERRYMAN, EDWARD JOHN - CAPTAIN DCM, CROIX de GUERRE
ROYAL FIELD ARTILLERY
King Street, Arundel

In 1918 Sergeant Major Berryman was promoted to Second Lieutenant; 'He had previously been awarded the DCM and the Croix de Guerre for Gallantry at Cambrai. He has been in France since the outbreak of war, except for home leave and is proud to be known as an old "Contemptible'. He was awarded the Military Cross in September 1918 having seen considerable service in the Army before the war and returned from India to take part in the present war, going to France in September 1914. Formerly with the Royal Horse Artillery he is now attached to the ammunition column of the Royal Field Artillery. Lieutenant Berryman is the youngest son of the late Mr and Mrs John Berryman, who were well known and esteemed in our district.

BERRYMAN, JAMES FREDERICK - PETTY OFFICER FIRST CLASS
HMS GOOD HOPE
Arundel
LOST AT SEA 1914

BERRYMAN, T - COASTGUARD
HM COASTGUARD SERVICE
In 1914 he was on wireless duty in Ireland
Brother of Lieutenant EJ Berryman and PO James Berryman (Lost at Sea)

BLACKMAN, ALFRED - SERGEANT
4th BATTALION ROYAL SUSSEX REGIMENT
Park Place, Arundel

BLACKMAN, B - PRIVATE
4th ROYAL SUSSEX REGIMENT
Arundel

BLACKMAN BERTRAM
2nd CANADIAN PIONEERS
Arundel
The son of Allen and Ellen Blackman, Bertram left England for Canada and returned with their forces when war broke out.
KILLED IN ACTION 28 OCTOBER 1918

BLACKMAN, E - PRIVATE
2 ROYAL SUSSEX REGIMENT
Arundel

BLACKMAN, GEOFFREY HAROLD - GUARDSMAN
GRENADIER GUARDS
Maltravers Street, Arundel

BLACKMAN, HARRY - PRIVATE
4th ROYAL SUSSEX REGIMENT
Tarrant Street, Arundel

BLACKMAN, PERCY - PRIVATE
4th ROYAL SUSSEX REGIMENT
Tarrant Street, Arundel
'Amongst the wounded 4th Battalion the Royal Sussex Regiment men in the Palestine fighting is Private P Blackman of Park Place. His relatives have been informed that he is in hospital in Alexandria suffering with a severe wound through his shoulder and a fractured arm'.
(May 1917)

BLACKMAN, RICHARD GEORGE - PRIVATE
ARMY SERVICE CORPS
Maltravers Street

BLACKMAN, SIDNEY - SERGEANT
1st SCOTS GUARDS
Park Place, Arundel
'Mr and Mrs Blackman, of Park Place, have received a card from their son, Sergeant Sidney Blackman informing them that he is a prisoner of war at Schneidemuhl, Germany, where he expects to remain till the end of the war. He says he is well and wishes to be remembered to all at home'.
PRISONER OF WAR

BLACKMORE - LANCE CORPORAL
ROYAL FUSILIERS
10 Rose Terrace, Arundel
DIED OF WOUNDS 1916
Not on War Memorial

BLACKMORE, HENRY - SGT MAJOR
10 Rose Terrace, Arundel
Peshawur Signal Division, India

BLAND, F - PRIVATE
3 ROYAL SUSSEX REGIMENT
Arundel
WOUNDED

BLUNDELL-INCE, BRET EDMUND - LIEUTENANT
ROYAL GARRISON ARTILLERY
Maltravers Street, Arundel

BLUNDELL-INCE, CECIL EDWARD - LIEUTENANT
ROYAL GARRISON ARTILLERY
Maltravers Street, Arundel

BLUNDELL-INCE, ERIC HENRY PHILIP - CAPTAIN
ROYAL GARRISON ARTILLERY

BOOKER, CLIFFORD THORBURN - SERGEANT
ROYAL ARMY SERVICE CORPS
Newburgh Arms, Tarrant Street, Arundel
Arundel

BOOKER, BERTRAM CHARLES - CORPORAL
DIVISIONAL EMPLOYMENT COMPANY
The Post Office, Ford Road
(Both Bert, above and Harry, below met unexpectedly behind the firing
line in May 1917)

BOOKER, HARRY JAMES - SERGEANT
LABOUR CORPS
The Post Office, Ford Road
The regular arrival each week of the West Sussex Gazette on the Front
Line was a source of comfort to many an Arundel soldier. In a letter dated
January 1918, Harry Booker wrote the following to the newspaper
expressing his appreciation;
'For nearly a year I have been receiving regularly from your office a copy
of the West Sussex Gazette and the pleasure that weekly messenger
provides is my justification for addressing this letter to you.

In this dreary wilderness of mud in which we flounder, far from any inhabited town or cultivated piece of land and where the monotony is only broken by the occasional visit of civilians from Britain, it is indeed pleasant to read of the homely doings in our lovely Sussex villages. Slindon and Graffham have added charms now, marvellous though they always were. I often call to mind the peaceful happy days I have spent in idle pleasure in our villages; especially do I picture them lying in their quiet seclusion, when my occupation out here takes me into wrecked and ruined villages all round the place from where I write, but not a single inhabitant is there, for there is not a house, a barn, a stable, or any building left standing. Churches, schools, all are levelled with the ground, or to be more literally correct, their sites are marked by heaps of bricks or stones. It is all very terrible and heart rending, but, with the help of Providence and the people at home, the perpetrators will be justly punished before long. While on this topic, may I be allowed to congratulate the writer of the weekly war article, for his clearness of vision and careful judgement when detailing events that happen out here. The articles are expressions of a carefully balanced opinion and incline neither to the extreme optimistic point of view, nor to the extreme pessimistic, both of which are nauseating to the soldier's taste. But yet they breathe great hope and that is the soldier's view. We are going to win, but it may be a longer "way to Tipperary" than 1914 thought possible.
The articles I have been referring to are read and appreciated here by men from the extreme points of Britain and all agree that they are splendid'.

BOSWORTH, ERNEST - PRIVATE
ROYAL ENGINEERS
High Street, Arundel

BOSWORTH, GW - LANCE CORPORAL
4th ROYAL SUSSEX REGIMENT
Arundel
'A member of the printing staff of the West Sussex Gazette, Lance Corporal Bosworth was 'honourably discharged from service' after serving one year and some eighty days fighting. He had contracted lung trouble and has been sent to a sanatorium in St Leonards. His official discharge says that Lance Corporal Bosworth "had proved a most excellent and reliable soldier. He is discharged in consequence of disease contracted while on active service in the Dardanelles'.
WOUNDED AND HONOURABLY DISCHARGED SEPTEMBER 1915

BRADEN, EDWARD - PRIVATE
ROYAL GARRISON ARTILLERY

BRASSFIELD, BENJAMIN CECIL - GUNNER
ROYAL FIELD ARTILLERY
Tarrant Street, Arundel

BRASSFIELD, FREDERICK GEORGE - PRIVATE
ROYAL ENGINEERS
Tarrant Street, Arundel

BRIDGER CHARLES - CORPORAL
19th HUSSARS
Orchard Place, Arundel

BROCKHURST, FREDERICK JAMES - PRIVATE
ROYAL ARMY SERVICE CORPS
High Street

BROWN, ARTHUR JAMES - LEADING SEAMAN
HMS CARDIFF
Arun Street, Arundel

BROWN, F - PRIVATE
ROYAL SUSSEX REGIMENT
Wounded July 1916
KILLED IN ACTION 1916
Not on War Memorial

BROWN, THOMAS HENRY - PRIVATE
MACHINE GUN SECTION BRITISH EXPEDITIONARY FORCE
Arun Street, Arundel

BUCK, WALTER - PRIVATE
4th ROYAL SUSSEX REGIMENT
The Lodge, Swanbourne Lake, Arundel
KILLED IN ACTION 26 MARCH 1917

BUDD, A - LANCE CORPORAL
4th ROYAL SUSSEX REGIMENT
In 1915 he was recovering in hospital in Malta from enteric and wounds

BUDD, WILFRED - LANCE CORPORAL
11th ROYAL SUSSEX REGIMENT
67Maltravers Street, Arundel
KILLED IN ACTION 1917

BUDD, COLIN LEONARD - PRIVATE
4th BATTALION THE NORFOLK REGIMENT
77 Maltravers Street, Arundel

BUDD, WILFRED ARTHUR - SERGEANT
4th ROYAL SUSSEX REGIMENT
Queen Street, Arundel
WOUNDED IN GALLIPOLI 1915

BUDDEN, FRANK WYATT
HMS BARHAM
7 Mountain View, Arundel

BULLER, PHILIP HENRY - PRIVATE
MACHINE GUN CORPS
Queen Street, Arundel

BULLER, TJ - PRIVATE
ROYAL ARMY SERVICE CORPS
Arundel

BURCH, A - PRIVATE
1st HERTFORDSHIRE REGIMENT

BURCH, AJ - PRIVATE
4th ROYAL SUSSEX REGIMENT
KILLED IN ACTION 1918

BURCH, CL - PRIVATE
4th ROYAL SUSSEX REGIMENT
Arundel

BURCH, ERNEST - PRIVATE
MACHINE GUN CORPS
1 California Terrace, Arundel

BURCH GEORGE CLEMENT - COMPANY SERGEANT MAJOR
4th ROYAL SUSSEX REGIMENT
Orchard Place, Arundel

In January 1916, Sergeant Major Burch wrote from Egypt thanking Mrs Wareham of the Arundel Co-operative Woman's Guild for the cigarettes they sent out 'to be distributed as far as possible among men coming from the Arundel district. Replying he wrote, 'I am sorry to say we have not many Arundel men with us now, but those that are here have benefited'. Later in the year; 'A prominent footballer and a staff member of the West Sussex Gazette, Sergeant-Major Burch was sent back to Blighty suffering from wounds to his head and neck'.

BURCH, GE - SERGEANT
ARMY VETERINARY CORPS
Arundel

A vet in civilian life, Private GE Burch, the son of Mr and Mrs Burch of Maltravers Street, enlisted in 1916 and because of his skills was promoted within a month, to Sergeant in the Army Veterinary Corps. He was originally stationed at Woolwich Barracks but went from there to France, where he had the harrowing job of dealing with often badly wounded horses. For the thirteen years prior to enlisting he had worked for Mr Pritchard, the Arundel Veterinary Surgeon and Veterinary Inspector for the West Sussex County Council at his practise Fitzalan Terrace, Station Road, Arundel.

BURCH, PERCY H - PRIVATE
9th EAST SURREY REGIMENT
South Marshes, Arundel

BURCH, RA - COMPANY SERGEANT MAJOR
1st HERTFORDSHIRE TERRITORIALS
South Marshes, Arundel

A former apprentice at the West Sussex Gazette, Sergeant Major Burch, whose parents once resided on South Marshes, was working at his trade in Hertfordshire when war broke out and volunteered immediately, leaving England in November 1914. He was made a Lance Corporal in November 1915 and within a fortnight became a Corporal, then a Sergeant in June 1916 and finally in May 1917 a Sergeant Major.

In March 1915 he wrote the following from a Flanders farmyard:
'I am still alive and kicking and must be thankful for these privileges as we are just now in a hot quarter. On 6 February I had the pleasure, if you can call it that, of witnessing an attack by our lads in the Brigade and splendid fellows they are, also a heavy bombardment of the German trenches by some two hundred of our guns. I can assure you it was a veritable inferno. On this particular day we did some good work with one of our machine guns. Then the following day (a Sunday) the Germans tried to have their own back and shelled our trenches, but although they dropped within a very few yards of our trenches their range was so bad that in the particular quarter there wasn't a single casualty for which many thanks. And so the game goes on! But we are slowly and surely nibbling them back'.

He then fought at Ypres, the Brickfields, Loos, the Somme and many other battles escaping injury, though foremost in the Machine Gun Corps, until taking part in the Battle of Messines Ridge, when he was hit in the left thigh by a shell fragment when taking Company Headquarters up to a captured German third trench. He was been Mentioned in Despatches for the prompt snubbing of a German counter attack which he 'stopped with his machine gun'.

In March 1918 he returned to Arundel and married Elsie Harpwood, Chichester lass, but did not have a long honeymoon as he was 'under orders to again proceed overseas at an early date'.

BURCH, WILLIAM JAMES - LANCE CORPORAL
WILTSHIRE REGIMENT
King Street, Arundel

BURCHELL, HENRY CHARLES - LANCE CORPORAL
4th ROYAL SUSSEX REGIMENT
Arun Street, Arundel

BURCHELL, WILFRED JOHN - PRIVATE
SUFFOLK REGIMENT
Arun Street, Arundel

BURCHER, JOSEPH WILLIAM CHARLES – SERGEANT
AVC
Causeway

BURCHER, R - PRIVATE
ARMY SERVICE CORPS
Causeway

BURCHER, WILLIAM - SERGEANT
ARMY VETERINARY CORPS
Causeway
'Rapid promotion has come to William Burcher, the son of Mr and Mrs WJ Burcher of Maltravers Street, who, after one month's service in the Army Veterinary Corps and has been made a Sergeant. He is now stationed at Woolwich, but will shortly proceed to France. Before enlisting Sergeant Burcher was for thirteen years employed as a vet with Mr Pritchard.

BURNS, WILLIAM GEORGE - GUNNER
ROYAL GARRISON ARTILLERY
River Road, Arundel

BURRELL, ARTHUR GORDON - PRIVATE
ALBERTA RESERVES
CANADIAN FORCES
Maltravers Street, Arundel

BURTON, JOHN - PRIVATE
AVC
Tarrant Street, Arundel

BUTCHER, R - PRIVATE
ROYAL ARMY SERVICE CORPS
Arundel

BUTCHER, RICHARD - PRIVATE
12th KINGS LIVERPOOL REGIMENT
Arundel

DIED IN FRANCE 1918

CALDWELL, FRANK - PRIVATE
WORCESTER REGIMENT
Tarrant Street, Arundel
PRISONER OF WAR

CALLOWAY, A - PRIVATE
ROYAL ARMY MEDICAL CORPS
Arundel

CAMPBELL, COLIN JOHN - LANCE CORPORAL
4th ROYAL SUSSEX REGIMENT
RIFLE BRIGADE
London Road, Arundel

CAMPBELL, DGH - CORPORAL
ROYAL SUSSEX REGIMENT
Arundel

CAMPBELL, J P - PRIVATE
ROYAL ENGINEERS

CAMPBELL, JH - PRIVATE
ROYAL NAVY

CAMPBELL, JP - SEAMAN
HMS AFRICA

CARPENTER, FRANK EDWARD - PRIVATE
ROYAL ARMY SERVICE CORPS
River Road, Arundel

CARR, GEORGE JOHN – PRIVATE
ARMY SERVICE CORPS
3 Wood View, Arundel

CARR, HENRY MARK - BANDMASTER
4th ROYAL SUSSEX REGIMENT
3 Wood View, Arundel

CARTER, W - PRIVATE
GRENADIER GUARDS
**REPORTED MISSING IN MARCH 1915, EX ARUNDEL POLICE
OFFICER**

CARTER, WILLIAM BLACKMAN - PRIVATE
ROYAL ENGINEERS
7 Kirdford Road, Arundel

CARVER, ALFRED GEORGE - BANDSMAN
ROYAL MARINES
HMS MONMOUTH
13 Ford Road, Arundel
LOST AT SEA 1 NOVEMBER 1914

CARVER, ALFRED WILLIAM - PRIVATE
4th ROYAL SUSSEX REGIMENT
15 Bond Street, Arundel
DIED OF WOUNDS 7 SEPTEMBER 1918

CARVER, CHARLES JAMES - CORPORAL
ROYAL SUSSEX REGIMENT
15 Bond Street, Arundel
Arundel Post Office Staff
KILLED IN ACTION – NOT ON WAR MEMORIAL

CARVER, ERNEST JAMES - SEAMAN
HMS VANGUARD
LOST AT SEA 9 JULY 1917

CARVER, FREDERICK - PRIVATE
ARMY ORDNANCE CORPS
15 Bond Street, Arundel

CARVER, GEORGE EDWARD - PRIVATE
ROYAL ARMY MEDICAL CORPS
Arun Street, Arundel

CARVER, J - LANCE SERGEANT
9th ROYAL SUSSEX REGIMENT
Arundel

CARVER, WALTER HERBERT - CORPORAL
Tarrant Street, Arundel

CHALCROFT, S
ROYAL SUSSEX REGIMENT
REPORTED MISSING SEPTEMBER 1916

CHALLEN, FREDERICK GEORGE - LANCE SERGEANT
ROYAL SUSSEX REGIMENT
94 Maltravers Street, Arundel

CHALLEN, HARRY JOSEPH - BATTERY SERGEANT MAJOR, LS & GC MEDAL
ROYAL GARRISON ARTILLERY
56 King Street, Arundel
DIED OF WOUNDS 12 MAY 1916

CHALLEN, JOHN ALFRED - LANCE CORPORAL
4th ROYAL SUSSEX REGIMENT
94 Maltravers Street, Arundel

CHANDLER, CECIL GEORGE - CORPORAL
ROYAL SUSSEX REGIMENT
Tarrant Street, Arundel

CHAPMAN, WILLIAM ALBERT - STOKER
ROYAL NAVY, DEVONPORT
Park Place

CHOWN, WILLIAM P - PRIVATE
4th ROYAL SUSSEX REGIMENT
River Road, Arundel
Arundel Post Office Staff

CHEESEMAN, JA - ACTING CORPORAL
ROYAL SUSSEX REGIMENT
WOUNDED 1916

CLANCHY, HENRY - SUB LIEUTENANT
HMS PRINCESS ROYAL

CLARK, ALFRED EDWARD
LABOUR CORPS DETACHMENT
129 Park Farm Cottages

CLARE, C - PRIVATE
ROYAL HORSE ARTILLERY
Arundel

CLARK, GEORGE - SERGEANT
MACHINE GUN CORPS
Orchard Place, Arundel
PRISONER OF WAR 1916

CLARK, JAMES FREDERICK - AIRMAN
ROYAL AIR FORCE
9 Verona Terrace, Arundel

CLARK, JF - PRIVATE
13th BATTALION ROYAL SUSSEX REGIMENT
Arundel

CLARK, LEONARD THOMAS - PRIVATE
2nd ROYAL SUSSEX REGIMENT
129 Park Farm Cottages, Arundel

Private L Clarke, the son of Mr and Mrs W Clarke, serving with the 2nd Battalion the Royal Sussex Regiment was wounded on October 7th in the Battle of Aisne and is in St Thomas's Hospital. His brother Private PJ Clarke is serving with the 8th Battalion of the same Regiment.

CLARK, THOMAS - PRIVATE
ROYAL WEST SURREY REGIMENT
Orchard Place, Arundel

CLARK, THOMAS HOWARD - PRIVATE
ROYAL SUSSEX REGIMENT
83 Surrey Street, Arundel

CLARKE, WB - STAFF SERGEANT
ROYAL ARMY ORDNANCE CORPS
Arundel

CLEAR, J G - PRIVATE
4th ROYAL SUSSEX REGIMENT
Arundel

CLEAR, JOSEPH PRIVATE
4th ROYAL SUSSEX REGIMENT
36 Bond Street, Arundel

CLEAR, WILLIAM EDWIN - PRIVATE
ROYAL GARRISON ARTILLERY
Maltravers Street, Arundel

CLEAR, JG - PRIVATE
4th ROYAL SUSSEX REGIMENT
Arundel

CLEMENTS, JOHN FREDERICK - PRIVATE
ROYAL ARMY SERVICE CORPS
10 Verona Terrace, Arundel,

CLEMENTS, JOSEPH - PRIVATE
SUFFOLK REGIMENT
20 California Terrace, Arundel

CLEMENTS, WILLIAM RICHARDSON - LANCE CORPORAL
4th ROYAL SUSSEX REGIMENT
Abercrombie Inn, Arundel
KILLED IN ACTION 19 APRIL 1917

CLEVETT, AS - PRIVATE
4th ROYAL SUSSEX REGIMENT
Arundel

CLIFTON, FRANCIS - PRIVATE
ROYAL ARMY SERVICE CORPS
Maltravers Street, Arundel

COLEMAN, FRANK WILLIAM - CAPTAIN MC
ROYAL FUSILIERS
Chichester Road, Arundel
'A commission as a Second Lieutenant has been granted to Corporal F
Coleman. He has served twenty years in the Army, went through the South
African campaign and after that married and went out to India, whence he
returned three years ago. He was stationed at Hounslow when war broke
out'.
June 1918; Captain Frank William Coleman, son-in-law of Mrs Suter of
Chichester Road has been awarded the Military Cross.
"On 25 March his Company to quote the official record, was holding a
"village on the Western Front which was heavily shelled and the company
came under very heavy machine gun fire. With absolute disregard to
personal safety, he rallied his men and re-organised the position and
greatly encouraged all ranks by his cheerful personality. Afterwards he
discovered an enemy machine gun in No Man's Land which was inflicting
casualties in the ranks of his Company. He immediately personally led a
Lewis gun team to within thirty yards of the enemy machine gun and with
great dash and determination he managed to kill the whole of the enemy
machine gun team and also destroyed the gun. This fine piece of work
undoubtedly saved a great number of casualties. The cool demeanour
shown by the Officer under fire throughout the recent operations has been

beyond all praise and he was continually organising schemes under shell and rifle fire to defeat the enemy".

COLEMAN, JOHN PHILIP - SERGEANT
COLDSTREAM GUARDS
59 Tarrant Street, Arundel

COLEMAN, HENRY JOSEPH - PRIVATE
1st EAST KENT REGIMENT
59 Tarrant Street, Arundel
KILLED IN ACTION 15 APRIL 1917

COLLIER, CALEB - GUNNER
ROYAL FIELD ARTILLERY, INDIA
Tarrant Street, Arundel

COLLINS, FREDERICK WILLIAM - PRIVATE
ROYAL ARMY SERVICE CORPS
Surrey Wharf, Arundel

COOK, GEORGE JOSEPH - PRIVATE
2nd ROYAL WEST SURREY REGIMENT
DIED OF WOUNDS 1917

CONSTABLE, GUY SEFTON - LIEUTENANT COLONEL MC
4th ROYAL SUSSEX REGIMENT
High Street, Arundel
Awarded the Military Cross in 1917
Captain Constable, the Mayor of Arundel, was the Commanding Officer of F Company, 4th Battalion, the Royal Sussex Regiment (Territorial's) and vacating his Mayoral position went to war with them. After a meeting, the Arundel Town Council issued a statement in which they;
'....regretted the absence of the Mayor, but we are proud that he should be doing his duty to his Country in command of the Arundel Company of his Regiment'.
Serving in the Dardenelles, he wrote the following letter to his successor as Mayor of Arundel in 1915:

'I am sitting at the bottom of a trench somewhere in Turkey. The Regiment went into action last Monday. They went into it like old soldiers. They are a Regiment to be proud of. Of course there were a lot of casualties, six or seven Arundel men and I have sent these names to my wife. I was lucky not to get hit as it was a pretty warm day, I can tell you.

It is poor fun sitting in a trench, as you do not dare to put your head up till dark and then it is not over safe. I expect we shall be in for a few days and then get a rest. We get very good bathing if we can manage it. The snipers are responsible for half the casualties; our Sergeant Drummer was killed last night. I managed to get a shave yesterday. I looked a pretty sight after a week without one! Please remember me to all the Town Council'.

Serving in Palestine in April 1917 Captain Guy Constable was slightly wounded but able to carry on with his duties. Three months later came the news that he had been awarded the Military Cross;

'All Arundel people will be delighted at the news that Captain Guy Constable, who it will be remembered was the Mayor of Arundel when war called him to sterner duties, has been awarded the Military Cross for service in connection with the severe fighting at the Battle of Gaza on March 26th and 27th. Details beyond the official announcement are not yet to hand, but it is evident from private sources that the award was most thoroughly deserved. When our advance was held up by the Company's fire he took the advance position with a small party and held out for the remainder of the day within a few yards of the enemy's trench under heavy fire and after himself being wounded. His initiative and gallantry were most marked. The warmest congratulations of the Town Council are to be conveyed to Captain Constable upon his having been awarded the Military Cross for Gallantry and Devotion to Duty on the Gaza battlefield. With the congratulations go the earnest hope for his speedy and safe return'.

August 1918; Lieutenant Colonel GS Constable MC who has been gazetted second in command of a Territorial Battalion of the Royal Sussex Regiment has been Captain of the 4th Battalion since 1913. He served with the volunteers in the South African War, 1900- 1902 and was awarded the Queens Medal with two clasps. For Gallantry in the present war he won the Military Cross., upon which honour he received the hearty congratulations of his fellow townsmen'.

COOPER, E - PRIVATE
4th ROYAL SUSSEX REGIMENT

COOPER, CV - PRIVATE
MIDDLESEX REGIMENT
Wounded 1917

CORBYN, PJ - PRIVATE
4th ROYAL SUSSEX REGIMENT
Arundel
A staff member of the West Sussex Gazette
WOUNDED IN 1915

Private Corbyn was a member of the printing staff of the West Sussex Gazette, who was wounded in the Gallipoli landings having received a rifle bullet in his neck. He was evacuated to England and transferred from Southampton to Graylingwell, Chichester by ambulance train. Having reached Havant Station where the train stopped, Private Corbyn surprised his brother who was on the station staff there, by introducing himself, through days of a bushy beard and standing in clothes which he had not been able to change for over a fortnight!

COUCHMAN, CW - SERGEANT DCM
REGIMENT UNKNOWN
'The parents of this distinguished young soldier are well known in the town, the father, a tailor, having been employed by Messrs. Watts and Nephew for many years and the mother, a member of the family of the late Mrs Rawlings of Arun Street.
Young Couchman has many "pals" in the town, who will be glad to hear of his distinction. It is interesting to note that his father saw active service in the Zulu and South African campaigns and although sixty years of age he rejoined the Colours in this war and is stationed at Dover'.
In October 1916, Colour Sergeant CW Couchman was mentioned in General Munro's despatches and awarded the Distinguished Conduct Medal. He has also had the Order of the Silver Star of Serbia conferred upon him.

COUSINS, JAMES - PRIVATE
6th FIELD SQUADRON, YEOMANRY
King Street, Arundel

CRANHAM, A H - PRIVATE
HMS KING GEORGE
Park Place

CRANHAM, EDWARD ALBERT - PRIVATE
2nd ROYAL SUSSEX REGIMENT
Park Place
DIED OF WOUNDS 1917

CRANHAM, ERNEST CECIL - SEAMAN
HMS KING GEORGE V
Park Place

CRANHAM, F J - PRIVATE
4th ROYALSUSSEX REGIMENT

CRANHAM, FRDERICK CHARLES - SEAMAN
HMS IRON DUKE
Park Place

CRANHAM, JAMES GEORGE – PRIVATE
10th HAMPSHIRE REGIMENT
Park Place, Arundel

CROWLEY, JOHN JOSEPH - PRIVATE
AVC
Arun Street, Arundel

CROWTHER, ARNOLD H - PRIVATE
SUSSEX IMPERIAL YEOMANRY
KILLED IN ACTION 24 FEBRUARY 1917

CUMMINGS, MONTGOMERY - PRIVATE
LINCOLNSHIRE REGIMENT
Tarrant Street, Arundel

CUMMINGS, RALPH - PRIVATE
11th ROYAL FUSILIERS
Tarrant Street, Arundel
Wounded in 1917
REPORTED MISSING 1918

CUTLER, AE - SERGEANT
ROYAL SUSSEX REGIMENT
REPORTED MISSING SEPTEMBER 1918

DAGGETT, ALBERT JOHN - PRIVATE
ARMY EMPIRE COMPANY
6th Kirdford Road, Arundel

DALTON, FELIX SAUNDERS - PRIVATE
MACHINE GUN COMPANY
High Street, Arundel,
An Arundel lad, Private Felix Dalton, the son of Mr Dalton of 7 Verona Terrace, who has been through the campaign in France and Flanders since Mons in August last year, has just been home on a weeks leave, to the great pleasure of his family, his friends and himself. He has come unwounded through many engagements and has had more than one lucky escape. At La Bassee for instance, a fragment of shell struck his rolled overcoat. It holed the cloth and knocked him down, but did no more injury. Again at Richebourg a shell burst over Private Daltons left shoulder, but left him unhurt, though it killed a man nearby. He can tell many stories of the Great War. Once, he and some comrades discovered a spy in a church belfry, who had a telephone wire which went through to a grave in the churchyard and communicated with the German trenches. The spy, an old woman, not a man in disguise was taken and shot. Spies are very numerous and tricked in khaki even penetrate the British trenches. (July 1915)

DALTON, LESLIE BENJAMIN - PRIVATE
10th ESSEX REGIMENT
High Street, Arundel
WOUNDED 1918

DALTON, JACK - SEAMAN
ROYAL NAVY
HMS RAGLAN
LOST AT SEA 1918

DALTON, REGINALD C - PRIVATE
ROYAL NAVY
HMS GRAFTON
HMS TIPPERARY
Arundel
LOST AT SEA 1916

DALTON, ROY L - LANCE CORPORAL DCM
ARMY CYCLIST CORPS THEN
6th LINCOLNSHIRE REGIMENT & HAMPSHIRE REGIMENT
Kings Arms Hill, Arundel

Writing to his parents in October 1915, Lance Corporal Dalton describes his experiences in Gallipoli:
'We have been in action for a month now and it has been the warmest time I have ever had in my life, both in the weather and circumstances. We had to force another landing here and by gum it was a landing. We had no sooner got to within two hundred yards of the shore when the bullets started pinging on the side of the boat, but luckily no one was hurt on our boat and as soon as our boys landed the fun began. It was just like a heavy shower of bullets and shrapnel, but our lads drove them for about two miles with fixed bayonets. They can't stand the cold steel. I had a bullet through the heel of my boot, it only just took the skin off my heel and a splinter of shrapnel grazed my skin, so you can see it is a pretty hot place, but it is a bit quieter now to what it has been'.
In July 1918 he was awarded the Distinguished Conduct Medal for 'gallantry on 6 June 1918'. He was by then serving with the Hampshire Regiment, Machine Gun Section. Whilst with the Hampshire Regiment he became the runner up in the Divisional boxing competition.

DAVIS, ERNEST RUEBEN - PRIVATE
LANCASHIRE REGIMENT
Tarrant Street, Arundel

DAVIS, WILLIAM - CORPORAL
4th R0YAL SUSSEX REGIMENT
Arundel

DAVIS, T - PRIVATE
4th BATTALION ROYAL SUSSEX REGIMENT
Wounded in Palestine 1917
Arundel

DEAN, ERNEST - PRIVATE
5th BATTALION THE ROYAL SUSSEX REGIMENT

In a letter to his sister in 1915 he wrote;

'You will be surprised to hear when I was on guard last night I heard a horse coming and when I stopped him, who should get off but Jim' (below).
They had not seen each other for three years. Ernest saw him again the next morning. They had both been laying in the same village for a week and not seen each other.

DEAN. JAMES - PRIVATE
15th HUSSARS
'Jim went out with the first Expeditionary Force; was through the Battle of Mons and the Aisne and at Ypres he lost his horse. He was cleaning the horse and hearing a shell coming managed to get out of the way just in time; his horse was killed. Since then, at La Basse, he was hit in the eye with a piece of shrapnel, but it has got alright again and his brother Ernest says he thought the life suited him, as he looked so well'.
WOUNDED 1916

DENYER, ARCHIBALD PERRY - LANCE CORPORAL
4th ROYAL SUSSEX REGIMENT
Maltravers Street, Arundel
Mr Frank Millam, of Maltravers Street, advertised in the columns of the West Sussex Gazette in February 1916. In June 1917 the newspaper cutting containing the advert was found by Private A Denyer, who wrote to Mr Millam:
'I do not know if you have received any applications from the Turks, but this was picked up not far from their lines!'

DENYER, CHARLES GEORGE - LANCE CORPORAL
3rd ROYAL SUSSEX REGIMENT
Maltravers Street, Arundel
KILLED IN ACTION 11917

DENYER, HE - PRIVATE
REGIMENT UNKNOWN

DENYER, WILFRED CLARENCE - PRIVATE
12th COMPANY ROYAL ENGINEERS
High Street, Arundel

DENYER WILLIAM HENRY - LANCE CORPORAL
4th ROYAL SUSSEX REGIMENT
Maltravers Street, Arundel
WOUNDED IN 1915 AND 1916

DIBLEY, RICHARD JAMES - ORDERLEY
ST JOHN'S AMBULANCE
Queen Street, Arundel

DIBLEY, WILLIAM EDMUND JAMES - PRIVATE
4th ROYAL SUSSEX REGIMENT
Queen Street
WOUNDED AT GALLIPOLI IN 1915

Before enlisting, Private Dibley worked for the West Sussex Gazette as an apprentice to the linotype. Now aged nineteen he had been a member of the 4th Battalion the Royal Sussex Regiment for two and a half years. In 1915 he took part in the landings at Gallipoli during which he received gunshot wounds to his right arm and was evacuated back to England, recovering at Graylingwell Hospital, Chichester.

During the landings in Gallipoli Private Dibley was in the firing line for about an hour before he was hit and stated that he never saw a Turk during that time, 'only a dead one'. Most of the injuries received by the Sussex men came from the Turkish snipers hiding in the cornfields. A measure of their effectiveness being highlighted by one Turkish sniper, who having been shot, was found to have in his possession the 300 Australian sovereigns and 80 allied soldiers identification discs. Even the Royal Army Medical Corps soldier who attended Private Dibley on the battlefield was shot in the arm by a sniper as he was dressing his wound.

'I am not sorry to see Sussex again', Private Dibley told the Littlehampton Observer reporter, although his convalescence was soon over and he returned to his Battalion.

Soon after his return he became ill and wrote home to say that he was getting better in November 1915;

'From the Mediterranean Field Force;

I am back with the boys. They are looking fairly well but say they have had a rough time which makes me think I was rather fortunate to have been injured on the first day. We are in dugouts now which seem fairly comfortable. There is something we hardly agree with and that is so many lodgers, hitchy coos. Of course it is a little exciting when the hunting begins. We are doing fatigues, digging out roads and trenches. It is fairly hard ground but the boys take it with a smile. Food is much better than one would expect and so enables you to carry on better. I hope Captain Constable got home alright for I hear he had a very trying time and I expect he feels he could do with the rest. Well I am just going sand lumping so must close'.

DORMAN, PETER MICHAEL - 2ND LIEUTENANT
6th BUFFS
Maltravers Street, Arundel

DUKE, REGINALD - GUNNER
ROYAL FIELD ARTILLERY
Arun Street

DUMBRELL, ARCHIBALD - SEAMAN
ROYAL NAVY
HMS VICTORY

DUNN, JJ - SERGEANT
4th ROYAL SUSSEX REGIMENT
Arundel

DUNWORTH, PATRICK JOSEPH - CAPTAIN
ROYAL ENNISKILLEN IRISH FUSILIERS
High Street

Patrick J Dunworth of the High Street, was serving with the 5th Connaught Rangers when he was evacuated to Cairo, Egypt, suffering from shock caused by the explosion of a poison gas shell near to him. He made 'an excellent recovery', returning to the fighting line within a few weeks and was granted his commission.
'Second Lieutenant Dunworth who is well known here, has seen some severe fighting in the Balkan campaign as well as in the earlier passages in Gallipoli. His technical sureness and smartness have been shown in many local undertakings and his well merited promotion will give him more extended opportunities to serve his Country'.
Promoted again, Captain Dunworth wrote to his wife. His letter is descriptive, powerful and poignant, telling of his last days on the Gallipoli Peninsula:

'For the last fortnight we have lived our lives over time and again. Crashing sounds of shot and shell, hails of bombs and bullets and plenty of shrapnel have gone on without ceasing over our position. We clung to our trenches when the shells wrecked them. The approaches over which I took up ammunition and food were paths of torment, torn and wrecked, every yard. The enemy's rifle and machine gun fire, beginning on a small scale increased tremendously as the days wore on. We stayed in our place for nine nights and days without relief or reinforcement, without much food and often without the time to prepare that which was bought up. Day after day the power of the enemy increased. Day after day the shells and bullets smashed into our lines. Day after day the number of shells and bullets increased. When it was seen that the enemy aimed at smashing the part of the line held by our Regiment, for three days every gun and rifle was turned on us. We beat back their infantry time after time, but could not stop the rain of shells. Every part of our position was torn day and night and was a wonder that any of us remained. Taking ammunition to the trenches, which was my job through the shooting was about as dangerous as could be wished. It was all no use they had twenty men to our one. More than once parties with me were blown away. Then came the enemy's final effort, finding as our fire grew slacker that our numbers were decreasing, the enemy gathered in thousands and in one mad powerful rush swept on to us. We killed them every yard. Our machine guns mowed them down until broken and we, fighting on the parapet, stood up to them with bayonets. They were fresh, whereas we had been exhausted by nine days hard digging and fighting. We had to withdraw to another position, fighting as we went. The last act in that position was to blaze off with revolvers into a crowd of the oncoming enemy. So we left our dead among the snows and are ready for another "go".
But the enemy does not seem too keen. Our machine gun men were great up to the last minute, when nearly all our machine guns were knocked out. But some of our best and bravest are asleep on the craggy hill-top and we will settle the account soon. You may get news of the battle in the papers or you may not, but the memory of it will live with us. And, later on, when round the fireside, I am telling you and the children about it, you will be able to realise how brave men die'.
In August 1917, then serving as a Lieutenant in the Royal Enniskillen Fusiliers, he was appointed Captain-Adjutant.
A year later in August 1918 he was reported as wounded in the head, ribs and hand in a telegram received by his wife. This was the seventh time he had been wounded.

EAMES, AG - PRIVATE
4th ROYAL SUSSEX REGIMENT
Tarrant Street, Arundel

A West Sussex Gazette printing staff member Private Eames was wounded in the knee in August 1915 and honourably discharged.

'Private Eames was wounded in the Dardenelles in 1915. As a result he was invalided out of the Army in March 1916, returning to civil life after war service which left him with a permanent stiff knee. As an apprentice printer Private Eames was one of the earliest volunteers to leave Arundel for the war and had seen active service at Sulva Bay. His Army discharge freed him 'in circumstances honourable to him'.

EDE, CECIL - PRIVATE
ROYAL ARMY MEDICAL CORPS
34 Bond Street, Arundel

EDWARDES ENT - SECOND LIEUTENANT
ROYAL FIELD ARTILLERY

In January 1917 Second Lieutenant Edwardes was granted a permanent commission in the regular Army, to date from 3 December 1916. He was previously a member of the literary staff of the West Sussex Gazette and volunteered at the outbreak of war.

ELLIS GP - SERGEANT MM
SUSSEX YEOMANRY
Arundel

It was announced on 21 March 1918 that Sergeant Ellis, who had been promoted several times since the outbreak of war had been awarded the Military Medal. He was transferred to the Machine Gun Section and had served in Gallipoli, Egypt and Palestine. He was also well known in Barnham where he worked.

ELLIS RG – SECOND LEIUTENANT
QUEENS ROYAL WEST SURREY REGIMENT
High Street, Arundel
WOUNDED AND DISCHARGED JULY 1917

We have seen with much interest many sketches sent home from France to his wife. They portray scenes in and about the trenches, buildings, the scenery of war and glimpses of the gallant fellows who are maintaining the honour of the old Country in the most stressful circumstances. Some of the sketches would certainly repay reproduction.

Ralph Gordon Ellis the son of an esteemed townsman, Mr WB Ellis who joined up at the wars outset and has passed his non commissioned grades (May 1917) and has been gazetted to Second Lieutenant. Returning to the Front with his new Regiment he was severely wounded by shrapnel in July 1917 which led to his being discharged from the Army as medically unfit.

ELLIS, TRAYTON - PRIVATE
Arundel
Ex Arundel Policeman and the father of Sergeant GP Ellis

ELLIS, WILLIAM PERCY - PRIVATE
4 ROYAL SUSSEX REGIMENT
Arundel

ELMS, ARTHUR - BANDSMAN
4th ROYAL SUSSEX REGIMENT
Arundel

ELMS, H - PRIVATE
ROYAL ENGINEERS
Arundel

ELMS, WALTER - CORPORAL
4th ROYAL SUSSEX REGIMENT

ELMS, WILLIAM - SERGEANT MAJOR
ROYAL ENGINEERS
Arundel

ETHERINGTON, ALBERT (BERTIE) - GUNNER
ROYAL GARRISON ARTILLERY
5 South Marshes, Arundel

ETHERINGTON, B - GUNNER
ROYAL GARRISON ARTILLERY
5 South Marshes, Arundel

ETHERINGTON, CHARLES EDWIN - PRIVATE
ROYAL ARMY MEDICAL CORPS
5 South Marshes, Arundel

Rushed home to England in 1915 for an emergency appendicitis operation
'An interesting story of how two Arundel brothers who have not seen each other for five years met on the battlefield in April 1917, is told in a letter from Charles Edwin Etherington serving with the Royal Army Medical Corps, of 5 South Marshes to his parents, Mr and Mrs William Etherington, at the same address. They have three other sons in His Majesty's Forces at the Front, William is in the Royal Army Service Corps, Edward is in Motor Transport, Albert is with the Royal Garrison Artillery, whilst their only daughter, Mary, is engaged in munitions work. Albert joined the Army some time before the war and had been stationed at Gibraltar, but the others all answered the Country's call at the commencement.

'You will be surprised', writes Win (Charles Edwin) 'that Bert and I have met at last. I hardly knew him, he has got a big chap. It was funny how we met. He took two men who had been killed into one of our dressing stations and he heard someone mention my lot. He asked where we were and they told him twelve miles away. So he got a lift over in a car. He arrived about six in the evening. I had just got in and was going to within a mile of his place. We went and had some food and I took him back in one of our cars. We had about four hours together and a talk about old times. I can tell you I felt it a bit to meet after five years a few yards from the line. He had a steel helmet on and a gas helmet ready the same as me. We never expected to meet like this and wondered if we would meet again. I hope he got over to his lot, he had to pass one place we call Demons Corner, but it was nice and dark. I am going to try and get over to him in a day or two. I cannot tell you how we both felt when we shook hands. I gave him Mary's letter. I have only Bill to meet and I have seen them all'.

He then went on to refer to two other Arundel boys:
'I know where young A Peskett (Royal Engineers) is. Tell his mother when she writes to send him the number of my lot and tell him to look out for me at the dump. He will know what I mean. Snooks, (Royal Sussex) who used to work at the Norfolk Hotel is quite well. We are not downhearted yet after two years'.

ETHERINGTON, EDWARD - PRIVATE
ROYAL ARMY SERVICE CORPS
5 South Marshes

ETHERINGTON, FREDERICK - SEAMAN
ROYAL NAVY
HMS ALBEMARLE
5 South Marshes

ETHERINGTON, WILLIAM - PRIVATE
ROYAL ARMY SERVICE CORPS
5 South Marshes, Arundel

EUSTACE, GEORGE WALLACE - CAPTAIN MC
ROYAL ARMY MEDICAL CORPS
Maltravers Street, Arundel

Captain Eustace Wallace was one of Arundel's Doctors engaged primarily on X-ray work. He was awarded the Military Cross for 'gallantry in severe fighting' in October 1917;
'He was going forward with a party which came under a very heavy barrage. He remained out in the barrage attending to the wounded, regardless of danger and carried one wounded man several hundred yards through the barrage to safety'.
Home on leave he attended a Town Council meeting and was heartily welcomed, the congratulations of his colleagues on the honour conferred upon him being felicitously voiced by the Deputy Mayor. Captain Eustace cordially acknowledged the compliment and spoke of the encouragement afforded local men who are serving in His Majesty's Forces by the knowledge that the town's affairs have been so efficiently conducted during the war.

FIELD, ARTHUR EDMUND - CORPORAL
ARMY PAY CORPS
Ford Road, Arundel

FIELD, FREDERICK - PRIVATE
ROYAL FIELD ARTILLERY
Arun Street, Arundel

FINCH, THOMAS JAMES - PRIVATE
NORTHAMPTON REGIMENT
Arundel

'Private T J Finch, formerly employed on the West Sussex Gazette linotype staff, now in a Lewis Gun section of the Northampton Regiment, came straight home on his first leave since he went out in September, 1916, straight from Passchendale Ridge and reported to our office here. Finch has been in some of the Somme battles and many of the later ones in Artois and Flanders and looks none the worse for it all. Mrs Finch and a little one doubtless made much of a fourteen days leave'.
He returned to England wounded in three places in March 1918 during the German Spring Offensive and was hospitalised in Bournemouth, where he was reported as doing well.

FLYNN, EDWARD - PRIVATE
RDC
Tarrant Street, Arundel

FLYNN, JAMES - SEAMAN
HMS DIANTHUS
HMS INVINCIBLE
Arundel
DIED AT SEA 1918

FLYNN, JOHN PATRICK - PRIVATE
13th BATTALION THE ROYAL SUSSEX REGIMENT
Arun Street, Arundel

FORD, ALFRED JOHN - PRIVATE
4th ROYAL SUSSEX REGIMENT
2 Mount Pleasant, Arundel

FOSTER, JOHN ROWLAND - PRIVATE
4th ROYAL SUSSEX REGIMENT
LABOUR CORPS
141 Chichester Road, Arundel

FOSTER, HL - PRIVATE
LABOUR CORPS
King Street, Arundel

FOSTER, L - PRIVATE
4th ROYAL SUSSEX REGIMENT
Arundel

FOULGER, LEONARD WILLIAM - FITTER
CROSSLEY'S AEROPLANE WORKS
1a London Road, Arundel

FREED, EDMUND HENRY - PRIVATE
2nd BATTALION ESSEX REGIMENT
Maltravers Street, Arundel

FREED, THOMAS - PRIVATE
3rd BATTALION COLDSTREAM GUARDS
Maltravers Street, Arundel

FREED, WALTER JOHN - PRIVATE
3rd BATTALION COLDSTREAM GUARDS
Maltravers Street, Arundel
PRISONER OF WAR

FRENCH, WILLIAM H - PRIVATE
1st ROYAL WEST SURREY REGIMENT
18 Chichester Road, Arundel
KILLED IN ACTION 1918

GALPIN, VIVIAN - GUNNER
ROYAL GARRISON ARTILLERY
Maltravers Street, Arundel

GAMMON, GEORGE WILLIAM
ROYAL SUSSEX REGIMENT
King Street, Arundel

GARDNER, ALFRED CHARLES - PRIVATE
ROYAL ARMY VETERINARY SERVICE
DIED IN FRANCE 1917

GARDNER, ERNEST HARRY - PRIVATE
23 AVC
Maltravers Street, Arundel

GARDNER F - PRIVATE
ARMY VETERINARY CORPS
Maltravers Street, Arundel,
DIED OF ILLNESS IN FRANCE 1917

GARDNER, WILLIAM - DRIVER
ROYAL ARMY SERVICE CORPS
Maltravers Street, Arundel,

GARTON, E - SERGEANT
Wounded July 1916

GEAR, CHARLES - PRIVATE
LABOUR CORPS
South Marshes, Arundel

GENT, EDMUND – SERGEANT
24th RIFLE BRIGADE
25 South Marshes

GENT, EDWARD - SERGEANT
RIFLE BRIGADE, INDIA
25 South Marshes
KILLED IN ACTION 1916

GERMANN, JOSEPH AMBROSE - SAPPER
ROYAL ENGINEERS
Maltravers Street, Arundel

GERMANN, PHILIP BERNARD - RIFLEMAN
LONDON REGIMENT
Maltravers Street, Arundel

GILBERT, FREDERICK - SEAMAN
ROYAL NAVY
HMS DONEGAL
Arundel Post Office Staff

GIBBINS, ERNEST GEORGE – PETTY OFFICER
ROYAL MARINE LIGHT INFANTRY
1 Wood View, Arundel

GILBERT, JACK – PRIVATE
ROYAL WEST KENT REGIMENT
Queen Street, Arundel

GILL, EDWARD - SECOND LIEUTENANT
6th ROYAL SUSSEX REGIMENT
Arundel

GILLHAM, FREDERICK – SERGEANT
ARMY SERVICE CORPS
5 Wood View, Arundel

GLOSSOP, AC
FRENCH AMBULANCE SERVICE
Arundel

GLOSSOP, BERNARD LAWRENCE - PRIVATE
ARMY PAY CORPS & WORCESTERSHIRE REGIMENT
High Street, Arundel

Private BL Glossop of the 2nd Worcestershire Regiment, was captured and taken prisoner of war in December 1914 and is working in a German Hospital. He had been reported as missing on September 20th. Mr and Mrs Glossop have two other sons serving, Sergeant PA Glossop, 'Q' Battery the Royal Horse Artillery and Private JFC Glossop who is with the 4th Cameron Highlanders. The following year it was reported;
'Mr W Glossop the fancy goods dealer of High Street, Arundel has received the welcome news that his son Bandsman Bernard Glossop of the Worcestershire Regiment who was taken prisoner at Mons arrived in

Switzerland on August 11th. Nothing had been heard of him for a long time, many letters having been returned, so the relief of his father and many friends will be readily appreciated. The news came through on a postcard from a Miss Luxton, who states that Bandsman Glossop has a running wound in his leg and has experienced a very hard time in Germany. She hopes that with the kind of treatment he will receive in Switzerland he will soon recover and everything will be done to make him happy and comfortable until the end of the war. Bandsman Glossop who joined the Army as a boy went to France with the Expeditionary Force and was captured by the Germans while he was attending to some British wounded'.

PRISONER OF WAR SEPTEMBER 1914

GLOSSOP, G - BANDSMAN
2 WORCESTER REGIMENT
Bradford House, High Street, Arundel

GLOSSOP, JOHN FRANCIS CHARLES - PRIVATE
4th CAMERON HIGHLANDERS
High Street, Arundel
Reputed to have been the first Arundel Territorial to see action at the Front, at Neuve Chapelle April 1915

GLOSSOP, PA - SERGEANT
ROYAL HORSE ARTILLERY
High Street, Arundel
Brother of Private BL Glossop and Private JFC Glossop met on the battle field after the Battle of Neuve Chapelle.

GLOSSOP, W
SOUTH AFRICAN UNION DEFENCE FORCE

GLOSSOP, WILFRED BERNARD - SERGEANT
ROYAL GARRISON ARTILLERY
High Street, Arundel
DIED OF WOUNDS 1916

GLOSSOP, WJ - CORPORAL
3 ROYAL SUSSEX REGIMENT
KILLED IN ACTION 1917

GOATCHER, GEORGE - PRIVATE
3rd LABOUR CORPS
ROYAL ARMY SERVICE CORPS
DIED IN FRANCE 1916

GOBLE, WILLIAM CHARLES - PRIVATE
LABOUR CORPS
High Street, Arundel

GODDARD, GEORGE ARTHUR - WRITER
ROYAL NAVY
Maltravers Street, Arundel

GOODACRE, RW - CORPORAL
SUSSEX YEOMANRY
Arundel

'News was received by his parents in June 1917 of the welfare of Corporal Goodacre, a member of the Chichester staff of the West Sussex Gazette who was wounded recently. His wound is a flesh one in the right thigh, caused by two shell fragments and that the bone, though painful is not broken. He is doing well in hospital in France'.
WOUNDED JUNE 1917

GOODALL, CHARLES HENRY - SAPPER
ROYAL ENGINEERS
Tarrant Street, Arundel

GRANT, RC - CAPTAIN
SCOTTISH RIFLES ATTACHED TO THE RAF
Arundel
Reported missing September 1918, lived at Wood End, Arundel, father a retired Army Captain.

GREEN, JH - LANCE CORPORAL
ROYAL ARMY MEDICAL CORPS
Arundel

Lance Corporal J H Green of the Royal Army Medical Corps was serving at a hospital in Seaford, Sussex. Having been promoted to Corporal he was removed to their depot in Aldershot, in November 1915.

GREENFIELD, A - PRIVATE
20 Gratefield Terrace, Arundel
ROLL OF HONOUR

This letter home in January, from Private A Greenfield, to his brother at 20 Gratefield Terrace, Arundel, followed his hearing of the death of another brother, Private F Greenfield of the 1st Scots Guards:
'We are up to our knees in mud I hope the weather will change soon I have lost about two stone. Poor Fred died as a soldier should, fighting for freedom and right. If it was not for such men as him England would have been under the German rule long ago. I think it is now up to every man to enlist, to keep the old flag flying.
Remember me to all and tell them I could do with a pint of Constables Ale, but no such luck at present. I hope someday to have a few together again in the dear old place'.

GREENFIELD, F - PRIVATE
1st SCOTS GUARDS REGIMENT
KILLED IN ACTION

GREENFIELD, JOHN WILLIAM HENRY - SERGEANT
High Street, Arundel

GREENFIELD, W - GUNNER
ROYAL FIELD ARTILLERY
Arundel

GREEST, JOHN - SAPPER
ROYAL ENGINEERS

GUNNER, ARTHUR HENRY EDMUND - SECOND LIEUTENANT
11th ROYAL SUSSEX REGIMENT
Bank House, High Street
KILLED IN ACTION 1918

GUNNER, GRACE MARGARET NURSE
WOMENS AAC
High Street, Arundel
Maltravers Street, Arundel

GUNNER, HENRY RAYMOND – SECOND LIEUTENANT
5th ROYAL IRISH REGIMENT
High Street, Arundel,
Lieutenant HR Gunner was originally a member of the Sussex Yeomanry and went to war with them. He was promoted through the ranks to Sergeant before being commissioned in Junev1916 and appointed to the Middlesex Regiment. In Arundel he was noted as being a 'popular and useful footballer' in the town team.

GUNNER, W - PRIVATE
3rd CITY OF LONDON YEOMANRY

GUNNER, WILLIAM HENRY - SECOND LIEUTENANT MC
60 (F) SQUADRON ROYAL FLYING CORPS
Maltravers Street, Arundel
KILLED IN ACTION 1918

GUSCOTT, FRANK - SERGEANT
10th ROYAL SUSSEX REGIMENT
Tarrant Street, Arundel

HAGGETT, ARTHUR ERNEST - SERGEANT
4th ROYAL SUSSEX REGIMENT
CITY OF LONDON FUSILIERS
Maltravers Street, Arundel

HAGGETT, JACK - PRIVATE
2 AM TRAINING SCHOOL
Maltravers Street, Arundel

HAGGETT, RICHARD AIRMAN
ROYAL AIR FORCE
Maltravers Street, Arundel

HAGGETT, WILLIAM - PRIVATE
4th ROYAL SUSSEX REGIMENT
Maltravers Street, Arundel
WOUNDED IN GALLIPOLI 1915

HALL, FREDERICK LOMAS - PRIVATE
AVC
Arun Street, Arundel

HAMMOND, ARTHUR HARRY - PLUMMERS MATE
HMS IMPERIEUSE
The Slipe, Arundel

HAMMOND, EDMUND HENRY - AIRMAN
ROYAL AIR FORCE
High Street, Arundel

HAMMOND, ERNEST CHARLES - CORPORAL
ROYAL ENGINEERS
High Street, Arundel

HAMMOND, FREDERICK K GEORGE - PRIVATE
8th ROYAL WEST KENT REGIMENT
ROLL OF HONOUR

HAMMOND, G - PRIVATE
4th ROYAL SUSSEX REGIMENT

HAMMOND, W - PRIVATE
ROYAL WARWICKSHIRE REGIMENT
Wounded 1916

HANKIN, CHARLES FREDERICK POWELL - STOKER
HMS EAGLET ROYAL NAVY
6 California Terrace, Arundel

HARDING, HENRY THOMAS - CORPORAL
11th CITY OF LONDON REGIMENT
Tarrant Street, Arundel
WOUNDED 1917

HARMAN AL - LIEUTENANT
ROYAL FIELD ARTILLERY
Orchard Place, Arundel

Lieutenant AL Harman served with the Royal Field Artillery. The son of Mrs Harman, of Orchard Place, Arundel, he wrote home from the Front early in September 1914 describing how when cornered he and his men escaped from the enemy:

'We are here resting for a few days, so I can just get a chance to write to you. I got your parcel today, thanks awfully and tell Rayner that the cigarettes were very welcome. Do you know we lost all tobacco and cigarettes on a wagon at Mons, where we had an awfully hot time and have been existing on goodness knows what ever since. Send as many as possible in the next parcel, also potted butter and meat please. No parcel may weigh more than 11 lbs.

Now I may tell you about Mons. We came into action on a very big hill just outside the village of Mesvin at about 11 o'clock on Sunday, the 23rd (August). I went to reconnoitre the position the night before; but it was a rotten bad position, but the only one. About 11 30 we shelled some infantry and I took my first series of active service; that is I directed the shooting of the battery. About midday they began to shell in and shelled us until 6 o'clock at the rate of about three hundred shells an hour over the 23rd Battery alone. But we had dug pits and were fairly safe, although they knocked out one man.

At 6 o'clock we had only fought a holding action; we were told the Germans, through weight of numbers were surrounding us, but we still had held them for six hours. We retired, one half of the battery going down one side of the hill and the other half, with the Major, Captain Lyster and myself, going down the other. Lyster had slight concussion. We got into a very narrow lane, where, from the steep banks we were fired on, ambushed at a range of about twenty yards. I was with the leading gun and my horses were shot down, the carriage turned sideways and so blocked the way forward. The lane was far too steep and narrow to turn round or to go back. We got out the gunners with rifles and drove the Germans back. I shot a man with my revolver as he was aiming at my lead driver. If the Germans had any initiative they could have scuppered us. Well, here we were, caught like rats in a trap. We built barricades and after dark the Major and I went scouting, while the remainder under Sergeant Clarke built barricades.

Lyster had already fainted three times in my arms. First we turned to the left and ran into a German patrol about a mile out, who, however, did not spot us. On the way back we heard firing and a party of Germans came rushing towards us; we crouched in the dark under a wall and so escaped their attention. They were men who had been driven off by the barricade. Next we went towards Mesvin, but ran into a German ammunition column, so came back; then we went about four miles to the right and ran into a body of troops whom we could not recognise till we heard an NCO say, "Walk March". We ran into the column with great joy and I hared back to tell the others, four miles away.

I will draw a veil over the rest of the night, trying and succeeding in getting the wagons out of the lane, over dead men and horses'.

HARRIS, HARRY - ACTING-CORPORAL
ROYAL ARMY SERVICE CORPS
30 King Street, Arundel

HARRIS, WILLIAM GEORGE – DESPATCH CLERK
WOOLWICH ARSENAL
High Street, Arundel

HARRISON, H - PRIVATE
4 ROYAL SUSSEX REGIMENT
Arundel

HART, E PRIVATE
ARMY VETERINARY CORPS
Arundel

HART, WILLIAM EDWIN - CORPORAL
ARMY VETERINARY CORPS

HARWOOD, ARTHUR E - SERGEANT MM
4th EAST KENT REGIMENT
Orchard Place, Arundel
Wounded in October 1915 and April 1917
Awarded the Military Medal in September 1917 'for bravery'

Sergeant Harwood was on leave when the awarding of his medal was announced. He joined the Army in 1915 and had been twice wounded. He married Miss Nora West of Fareham during his weeks leave.
Sergeant Arthur Harwood of the Buffs (East Kent Regiment) the son of Mr and Mrs Harwood of Orchard Place has won the Military Medal for bravery. He has been home on leave this week after nearly two years service at the Front and was married to Miss Nora West of Fareham. Sergeant Harwood joined the Army in 1915. He has been twice wounded, once at Loos in October 1915 and again at Arras in April 1917.

HARWOOD, AH - PRIVATE
2nd ROYAL FUSILIERS

HARWOOD, EDMUND JOHN - PRIVATE
R.A.O.C.
London Road, Arundel
Town postman prior to enlisting
WOUNDED IN 1916

HARWOOD, F - PRIVATE
MIDDLESEX REGIMENT
Arundel

HARWOOD, JAMES CORPORAL MM - ACTING LANCE SERGEANT
4th ROYAL SUSSEX REGIMENT
Orchard Place, Arundel
Arundel Post Office Staff
KILLED IN ACTION 1918

HARWOOD, T - PRIVATE
REGIMENT UNKNOWN

HARWOOD, WILFRED FRANCIS – PRIVATE
588th LABOUR COMPANY
6 California Terrace, Arundel

HARWOOD, WILLIAM FRANCIS - PRIVATE
ROYAL FUSILIERS
London Road, Arundel
WOUNDED IN JULY 1916

HAYLOR, GEORGE EDWARD
2 AM SCHOOL OF NAVIGATION
5 Greystock Terrace, Arundel

HAWKES, FREDERICK VINCENT - PRIVATE
ROYAL ENGINEERS
Tarrant Street, Arundel

HAYES, ARTHUR JAMES - PRIVATE
2nd ROYAL SUSSEX REGIMENT
KILLED IN ACTION 1915

HAYWOOD, AH - ROYAL FUSILIERS
Arundel

HEALY, HENRY - LANCE CORPORAL
MILITARY FOOT POLICE
55 King Street, Arundel

HENSON, PHILIP - PRIVATE
ROYAL WEST SURREY REGIMENT
4 Arun Cottages, Arundel
PRISONER OF WAR

HERBERT, J
CAPE MOUNTED POLICE
Arundel

HERBERT, JACK - PRIVATE
4th ROYAL SUSSEX REGIMENT

'The wife of Private Jack Herbert has received intimation that her husband has been seriously wounded in France. Jack Herbert, who was the Butler to the late Colonel EJ Mostyn, has many friends in Arundel, where, some few years ago, he was a familiar and popular member of the football team. The extent of his injury is not yet known, but it is described as serious and prayers were offered on his behalf at St Philip's Church on Sunday.

HERBERT, PHILIP JOHN - PRIVATE
4th ROYAL SUSSEX REGIMENT
2nd WILTSHIRE REGIMENT
17 California Terrace, Arundel
HOSPITALISED IN MALTA SUFFERING FROM ENTERIC CONTRACTED AT GALLIPOLI

HERSEE, WALTER JAMES - SERGEANT
4th ROYAL SUSSEX REGIMENT
St Mary's Gate Inn, London Road, Arundel
Sergeant Hersee was wounded in March 1917, 'the bullet passed through his helmet and shoulder and out through his right arm.
**SERIOUSLY ILL WITH ENTERIC SEPTEMBER 1915
WOUNDED MARCH 1917 AND AGAIN IN NOVEMBER**

HILL, SYDNEY MONTAGUE HARDWICK - PETTY OFFICER
HMS PRINCESS IRENE
LOST WHEN SHIP BLEW UP 1915

HILLS, JT - PRIVATE
4th ROYAL SUSSEX REGIMENT
Arundel
TWICE WOUNDED IN JULY 1915

HOATHER, H - PRIVATE
ROYAL SUSSEX REGIMENT
REPORTED MISSING IN 1917

HOATHER, THOMAS WILLIAM - PRIVATE
LABOUR CORPS
8 California Terrace, Arundel

HOLDEN, CHARLES ELBEN - PRIVATE
2nd ROYAL SUSSEX REGIMENT
Queen Street, Arundel

HOLDEN, RUDOLPH - PRIVATE
18th BATTALION GLOUCESTER REGIMENT
Queen Street, Arundel

HOLDSTOCK, C - GUARDSMAN
GRENADIER GUARDS
Arundel
Former Arundel Police Constable
WOUNDED AND PRISONER OF WAR

HOLLOWAY, ALBERT JAMES - CORPORAL
ARMY VETERINARY CORPS
Maltravers Street, Arundel

HOLMES, R - SECOND LIEUTENANT
9th SOMERSET LIGHT INFANTRY
Arundel

HORNSEY, THOMAS - PRIVATE
PRISONER OF WAR

HORSLEY, J - PRIVATE
3rd ROYAL SUSSEX REGIMENT
Arundel

HOWARD, GR - GUNNER
ROYAL FIELD ARTILLERY
Arundel

HOWARD, HARRY - CORPORAL
RDC
Tarrant Street, Arundel

HULLS, ARCHIBALDS EDGAR - PRIVATE
ARMY VETERINARY CORPS
High Street, Arundel

HULLS, RICHARD WILLIAM JNR - SECOND LIEUTENANT
ROYAL SUSSEX REGIMENT
The Causeway, Arundel

HUMPHREY, M - PRIVATE
ROYAL SUSSEX REGIMENT
WOUNDED JULY 1916

HUNT, CHARLES JAMES - PRIVATE
MIDDLESEX REGIMENT
Tarrant Street, Arundel

IDE, ALBERT WALTER – PRIVATE
ROYAL ARMY MEDICAL CORPS
The Foundry, Ford Road

JACOB, HL PRIVATE
8TH (CYCLIST) ESSEX REGIMENT
Arundel

JARVIS, A E - PRIVATE
1st DUKE OF WELLINGTON'S
WEST RIDING REGIMENT
7 Dunromin Terrace, Ford Road, Arundel

Sent home in 1915 with malaria, to Southampton Hospital; on returning to the Front he wrote thanking the West Sussex Gazette for sending copies of the newspaper to him;
'I am now in the best of health and it is a lot better this time than the first in regard to supplies, but we have a good bit of mud. Note when we get back for a rest we have the chance for a hot bath and a change of underclothing, which is a good relief'.

JARVIS, WALTER - PRIVATE
1st DUKE OF WELLINGTONS REGIMENT
7 Dunromin Terrace, Ford Road, Arundel
**HOSPITALISED BACK IN SOUTHAMPTON WITH A SERIOUS
FEVER NOVEMBER 1914**

JENKINS, H - PRIVATE
SUSSEX IMPERIAL YEOMANRY
Arundel

JOHNSON, ALFRED JOHN - PRIVATE
15th LONDON REGIMENT
2a Kirdford Road, Arundel
KILLED IN ACTION 1918

JOHNSON, CW - PRIVATE
4th ROYAL SUSSEX REGIMENT
Arundel

JOHNSON, J - PRIVATE
4th ROYAL SUSSEX REGIMENT
Arundel
WOUNDED IN PALESTINE MAY 1917

JOHNSON, J - PRIVATE
ROYAL GARRISON ARTILLERY

JOHNSTONE, R WRITER
ROYAL NAVY
HMS VICTORY

JONES, AE - GUARDSMAN
GRENADIER GUARDS
Arundel
AN EX ARUNDEL POLICEMAN WOUNDED IN 1915

JONES, CF - PRIVATE
7th EAST KENT REGIMENT
KILLED IN ACTION 1916

JONES, JOSEPH EDWARD - PRIVATE
AVC
Queen Street, Arundel

JONES, TE
ROYAL NAVAL FLYING CORPS

C VIVIAN, JONES – DESPATCH RIDER
KENT CYCLE BATTALION, MOTOR CYCLE SECTION
Commerce House, Arundel
Mr and Mrs Frank Jones have received information from the War Office that their son, C Vivian Jones has been missing since 30 September last. Although still in his teens, he had served his country since the outbreak of war, having put up his age to serve as a Despatch Rider; in July last he was hastily sent to France and attached to the 7th Buffs.
Mr and Mrs Jones wish to thank all those who have shown them much kindness during the suspense through which they are passing.

JORDAN, A - RIFLEMAN
RIFLE BRIGADE
WOUNDED IN 1916 AND 1917

JUDD, WILLIAM SYDNEY - SAPPER
ROYAL ENGINEERS
DIED AFTER WAR 1919

JUPP, AJ - PRIVATE
4th ROYAL SUSSEX REGIMENT
Arundel

JUPP, AJ - GUNNER
ROYAL GARRISON ARTILLERY

KATES. SC - PRIVATE
3rd ROYAL SUSSEX REGIMENT
Arundel
Wounded July 1916

KATES, SIDNEY C - PRIVATE
ROYAL SUSSEX REGIMENT

KENDALL, ARTHUR ELLIS AUGUSTINE - PRIVATE
4th ROYAL SUSSEX REGIMENT
KILLED IN ACTION 1915

KENDALL, FRANCIS GERALD - PRIVATE
4th ROYAL SUSSEX REGIMENT
The Causeway, Arundel
WOUNDED IN PALESTINE MAY 1917

KENDALL, WILLIAM LLEWLLYN – ACTING CORPORAL
ARMY ORDNANCE CORPS
12 Kirdford Road, Arundel

KENT, GEORGE ARTHUR - PRIVATE
SPECIAL MOBILE WIRELESS STATION, DARDONI,
NORTH WEST FRONTIER
30 King Street, Arundel

KENT, WILLIAM FRANCIS
6th ROYAL WARWICKSHIRE REGIMENT
KILLED IN ACTION 1917

**KENWARD, ERNEST GEORGE - LANCE CORPORAL
DRUMMER**
7th ROYAL SUSSEX REGIMENT
Arun Street, Arundel

KENWARD, HENRY CHARLES - 1ST CLASS STOKER
HMS HAMPSHIRE
Arun Street, Arundel
LOST AT SEA 1916

KENWARD, JAMES WILLIAM - PRIVATE
ROYAL SUSSEX REGIMENT
19 Arun Street, Arundel
KILLED IN ACCIDENT AT HOME 1916

KERR, MALCOLM HAROLD - CORPORAL
LONDON REGIMENT
7th River Road, Arundel

KERR, REGINALD - PRIVATE
4th ROYAL SUSSEX REGIMENT
River Road, Arundel
KILLED IN ACTION MARCH 1917

KING, ARTHUR JAMES – CORPORAL
5 R.B.R.D.C.

KING, GEORGE - GUNNER
HAMPSHIRE REGIMENT
ROYAL FIELD ARTILLERY

KING, L -ROYAL MARINE LIGHT INFANTRY

KING, WB - RIFLEMAN
UPPER BURMA FRONTIER GUARD MOUNTED RIFLES
Arundel

KINNARD, AA - SIGNALLER
ATTACHED TO THE WORCESTER REGIMENT

Signaller A Kinnard, formerly in the estate employ, now attached to the Worcester's somewhere in France, writes cheerily that he has not many

Sussex boys near him, he wishes he had, but always enjoys reading the War Special of the West Sussex Gazette and feels his friends will 'be pleased to hear that I am getting on well out here'.

KIY, G - GUNNER
ROYAL FIELD ARTILLERY

KNOWLES, WILLIAM - PRIVATE
QUEENS REGIMENT
King Street, Arundel

LAKE, PERCY JOHN - CORPORAL MM
4th ROYAL SUSSEX REGIMENT AND
NORTH LANCASHIRE REGIMENT
Mount Pleasant, Arundel

The son of Mr Chas. Lake, foreman of the Corporation employees, Lance Corporal Lake has been awarded the Military Medal and promoted to the rank of Corporal. The award is for "bravery and devotion to duty during an intense bombardment and an attack on the enemy".

LANDER, T – SHOEING SMITH
ROYAL ENGINEERS
Arundel

LAVERTY – INFANTRY MAN
DUKE OF CORNWALL'S LIGHT INFANTRY
Arundel

LAWRENCE, A - PRIVATE
4th ROYAL SUSSEX REGIMENT

LAWRENCE, WILFRED HENRY - PRIVATE
TANK CORPS
Hiorne Tower, Arundel Park, Arundel

LEE, JOHN WESTON - PRIVATE
4th ROYAL SUSSEX REGIMENT
12 Mount Pleasant, Arundel
WOUNDED IN GALLIPOLI MAY 1917

LEE, WILFRED JOSEPH - PRIVATE
ROYAL ARMY SERVICE CORPS
12 Mount Pleasant, Arundel

LEE, MICHAEL PHILLIP - PRIVATE
1st MIDDLESEX REGIMENT
12 Mount Pleasant, Arundel
DIED AT HOME 1918

LEE, WILLIAM - PRIVATE
ARMY SERVICE CORPS
12 Mount Pleasant, Arundel

LEGG, HWG - PRIVATE
Arundel Post Office Staff

LEGGETT, GEORGE - PRIVATE
4th ROYAL SUSSEX REGIMENT

LEWINGTON, ERNEST VICTOR - PRIVATE
7th ROYAL SUSSEX REGIMENT
KILLED IN ACTION 1918

LIGHT, EW - PRIVATE
9th ROYAL SUSSEX REGIMENT
22 California Terrace, Arundel

LIGHT, HERBERT BURCH - AIRMAN
22 California Terrace, Arundel
ROYAL AIR FORCE

LIGHT, HORACE - PRIVATE
CAMERON HIGHLANDERS
22 California Terrace, Arundel

LIGHT, SIDNEY CHARLES - SERGEANT
ROYAL AIR FORCE
22 California Road, Arundel

LIPSCOMBE, CF - PRIVATE
3rd ROYAL SUSSEX REGIMENT
South Marshes, Arundel
WOUNDED NOVEMBER 1914

LOUDON, MARCUS GEOFFREY - SECOND LIEUTENANT
KING EDWARDS HORSE
Arundel

LOVE, FREDERICK – PRIVATE
LABOUR CORPS
5 Kirdford Road, Arundel

LOVELOCK, GE - PRIVATE
8th (CYCLIST) ESSEX REGIMENT

LOVELOCK, WJ- CORPORAL
7th ROYAL WEST KENT REGIMENT

LUCAS, AP - PRIVATE
1st ROYAL SUSSEX REGIMENT

LYNN, ALFRED CHARLES - PRIVATE
4th ROYAL SUSSEX REGIMENT
Surrey Street, Arundel

LYNN, ARTHUR - PRIVATE
THE BUFFS
24 Bond Street, Arundel

LYNN, CHARLES FRANK - PRIVATE
IRISH GUARDS
KILLED IN ACTION 1918

LYNN, FRANCIS SEFTON - PRIVATE
ARMY SERVICE CORPS
Surrey Street, Arundel

LYNN, ROBERT – PRIVATE
19th MIDDLESEX, ARMY OF THE RHINE
24 Bond Street, Arundel

LYNN, WT - PRIVATE
4th ROYAL SUSSEX REGIMENT

MALLARD, HENRY GEORGE
CANADIAN ARMY SERVICE CORPS
Maltravers Street, Arundel

MATES, ARTHUR JAMES - GUNNER
ROYAL FIELD ARTILLERY
South Marshes, Arundel

MARCUS, GEOFFREY LOUDON - TROOPER
KING EDWARDS HORSE

MARTIN, CLAUDE EDWARD
MERCANTILE MARINE
Maltravers Street, Arundel

MARTIN, W - PRIVATE
MIDDLESEX REGIMENT
Wounded July 1916

MARTIN, W SNR - PRIVATE
NATIONAL RESERVE
On duty with the Arundel detachment guarding the London to Dover
railway line in 1914

MARTIN, WH - CORPORAL
4th ROYAL SUSSEX REGIMENT

MATES, ARTHUR JAMES – GUNNER
12th FIELD ARTILLERY
South Marshes, Arundel

MATES, EW - GUARDSMAN
COLDSTREAM GUARDS
INVALIDED AND DISCHARGED

MAXWELL-STUART, ALFRED JOSEPH
SECOND LIEUTENANT - GUARDSMAN
1st COLDSTREAM GUARDS
Batworth Park, Arundel
DIED OF WOUNDS

MAXWELL-STUART, EDMUND JOSEPH - LIEUTENANT
ROYAL ENGINEERS
Batworth Park, Arundel
KILLED IN ACTION

MAXWELL-STUART, HENRY JOSEPH IGNATIUS
SECOND LIEUTENANT - GUARDSMAN
3rd COLDSTREAM GUARDS
Batworth House, Arundel
KILLED IN ACTION 1916

MAXWELL-STUART, JOSEPH JOHN - LIEUTENANT
9th DUKE OF WELLINGTONS REGIMENT
KILLED IN ACTION 1916

MERRIOTT, WC - GUNNER
ROYAL FIELD ARTILLERY

MERRIDEW, CHARLES - PRIVATE
4th ROYAL SUSSEX REGIMENT
Kirdford Road, Arundel
KILLED IN ACTION 1917

MERRIDEW, HAROLD - PRIVATE
13th ROYAL SUSSEX REGIMENT
Kirdford Road, Arundel
KILLED IN ACTION 1917

MILLS, AE - PRIVATE
2nd ROYAL SUSSEX REGIMENT
Arun Street, Arundel
WOUNDED IN 1914 AND 1916

MILLS, ALFRED SNR - PRIVATE
LABOUR CORPS
Arun Street, Arundel

MILLS, E - PRIVATE
HAMPSHIRE REGIMENT
Wounded 1916

MILLS, GEORGE ARTHUR - LANCE SERGEANT
12th ROYAL SUSSEX REGIMENT
KILLED IN ACTION 1917

MILLS, GEORGE WILLIAM – PRIVATE
ROYAL ARMY MEDICAL CORPS
Maltravers Street, Arundel

MILLS, EO - SERGEANT
4th ROYAL SUSSEX REGIMENT

MILLS, GAH - PRIVATE
4th ROYAL SUSSEX
Arundel Post Office Staff

MILLS, HARRY - LANCE CORPORAL
5th BATTALION ROYAL SUSSEX REGIMENT
King Street, Arundel

MILLS, HARRY - SAPPER
9th FIELD COMPANY, ROYAL ENGINEERS
ATTACHED TO THE
4th ROYAL SUSSEX REGIMENT
Lower Parade, Arundel
KILLED IN ACTION 1914

MILLS, R - PRIVATE
4th ROYAL SUSSEX REGIMENT
Lower Parade, Arundel

MITCHELL, RF - CAPTAIN
4th ROYAL SUSSEX REGIMENT
Arundel
Junior proprietor of the West Sussex Gazette

MOFFATT, WJ - TROOPER
SUSSEX YEOMANRY

MOODY, WJ - GUARDSMAN
COLDSTREAM GUARDS
Reported missing 1916

MOORE, ALFRED GEORGE - PRIVATE
ESSEX YEOMANRY
River Road, Arundel

MOORE ERIC PRIVATE
4th ROYAL SUSSEX REGIMENT
River Road, Arundel

MORLEY, HAROLD - PRIVATE
2nd ROYAL SUSSEX REGIMENT
7 Gratwicke Terrace, South Marshes, Arundel

'Several Arundel men at the Front have been wounded, one, Harold Morley, a chorister at St Nicholas Church, of 7 Gatwick Terrace of the 2nd Battalion, the Royal Sussex Regiment lies in Birmingham Hospital'. That news in September 1914 was the first report of Arundel men being wounded; Private Harold Morley was a regular soldier, serving with the 2nd Battalion, the Royal Sussex Regiment. He was evacuated back to England, where he wrote home from hospital:
'I am getting on alright. We are all well looked after, the hospital is in Birmingham University. We went from Southampton to Le Havre and the first thing that attracted my attention was the comical dress of the French soldiers. They wear great blue coats and red trousers and if you saw them marching along in England you would think it was a circus procession or something of that sort. We stopped at Le Havre for one day and continued on the following midnight by train. We must have travelled two or three hundred miles past Amiens and Arras and got out at a small station called Wassigny. We stopped at all the large stations and there were crowds of people on the platforms with loaves of bread, cigarettes, tobacco, milk, cider, eggs boiled, chocolates and all kinds of fruit. It was a glorious time for us all until we got to a small village called -------. We stopped there for five days and from there we were on the march day and night. Owing to aeroplanes we could not go into billets until after dark and we had to be away before light. We reached as far as Mons but we did not get into actual fighting with them. I happened to be an eye witness, that was the first time I had seen such a sight.
The next day we had to start the retirement. We must have marched a good thirty miles and to make things worse it was raining all afternoon and evening. We had our overcoats in our packs and that's where they stopped, we had no order to take them out. We got into a village about 9pm that night, soaking wet and clinging to us, we hardly knew how to get along. We were given a waterproof sheet each which we had handy if it came on to rain. Our Brigade went right through Soissons and Collumers. But the thing that was most distressing was to see the poor refugees leave their homes. We could not get any bread now, one baker was asked for bread and could speak English said it was no use getting fresh supplies in and making more bread for the Germans to take. We had to live on corned beef

and hard biscuits like dog biscuits. When we started the advance we saw nothing but deserted villages with all the shops and villages utterly pillaged.

Has Mrs Dalton heard anything from Felix? (Private Felix Dalton, 2nd Battalion the Royal Sussex Regiment). I saw him two hours before I got wounded, that was about 10am on 10 September. The Battalion that morning walked right into a death trap. The German Artillery was firing at us from a range of 450 yards. Shells were bursting over us like drops of rain. Our three heads were all killed, the Colonel, Adjutant and Regimental Sergeant Major. But of Felix or any of the others from Arundel I know nothing, but I hope they are alright.

I have not told you much about the day I got wounded. It was the 10 September, a Thursday, the Battle of the Marne, last day. I will try to tell you practically what happened. We were on the march long before it was light. We knew we were hot on the heels of the Germans and so expected to come into contact with them during the day. We had gone about ten miles when in the distance on a line of hills on the skyline we could see small batches of German cavalry moving about. As we got closer they all retired. That day our Battalion was leading the column. To be able to advance over the hill the first three Companies went up in extended order, 'A' company being the last. We were the first to go up in column; that is in fours. As the first three Companies reached the top shrapnel shells came and burst over the top of us like rain. At this first outset we all darted to the left of the road under cover of a ridge. The first three Platoons were ordered to advance in extended order, our Platoon again being the last. Before the order came for us to extend a shell burst in the middle of us and I swear that when the order did come there were no more than 20 out of 50 complied with it. I laid there among the dead and wounded. I could not walk until I was properly dressed and cared for a bit. I got a shrapnel bullet in the back and it is still there. I had it X-Rayed last evening and will probably have it taken out tomorrow (Friday). The shells are about a foot long and contain 364 bullets. They are timed to burst in the air and the forward throw is 200 yards by 75. That is to say if a shell bursts over the top of me anyone within a distance of 200 yards is likely to be shot down'.

Private Morley had extended sick leave before re-joining his Regiment. Miss Bishop, of Maltravers Street, Arundel, received the following letter from Signaller H Morley of 2nd Battalion the Royal Sussex Regiment in October 1915, which bought a fair amount of bad news:

'We have for the last ten days been in the thickest of the fighting in the latest British advance. How I have been able to get through it all I do not know. The Germans were very active with their artillery they had every road, trench and prominent object ranged to the very yard. The narrowest escape I had was a week ago yesterday. There were seven of us Royal Sussex together having a chat when shrapnel burst not more than six yards from us, hitting four with two very seriously injured. How all the three hundred bullets which came from that shell missed me I do not know, I thought my time had come, but here I am still merry and bright.

We gave the Germans something to remember. Our Brigade captured about seven hundred unwounded prisoners and penetrated the German lines by about two miles. The weather was a great setback to us, it rained every day for hours at a time and we had no cover. I have been wet through three times during the last week and the nights have come on and they have been bitterly cold. I should be very grateful if you could send me a muffler and a pair or two of socks. Owing to so much rain the mud and water in the trenches is over the tops of our boots and it is a treat to have a pair or two of spare socks to change at every opportunity as we are rarely in a position to be able to wash and dry those we have taken off.

Felix Dalton is still quite well and wishes to be remembered to yourself and Mrs Bishop. But I'm afraid we have lost one Arundel man and I am trying to get any information I can of poor Percy Rowe. His Company Sergeant Major told me he had been killed and a chum of his in his Company said he saw him lying down face upwards not more than twenty yards from the German wire entanglements. I cannot say he has been killed as I did not see him myself. I should be only too pleased if it were not true as he was a good friend and a chum to me and I miss him very much.

Two Arundel men have been wounded, Corporal Denyer and Edward Cranham and Fred Sturt has got gassed from poisonous gas shells. I do not know if it was serious or not. I got a slight taste of it myself, it made my eyes smart awfully but I have got over it alright. We are having a rest for a few days, a well earned rest. For eight days none of us had a whole nights rest and we are all pretty well worn out.

I came across another Arundel man today who is in the Royal Field Artillery. I do not know if you remember him or not. Before he enlisted he worked behind the counter for Watkins and Co, grocers in the High Street. His name is Laker, sorry I should have said Mr Laker, but of course in the Army we speak of them by the rank they hold and as a Private we go by our surnames. I expect we shall hear a little bit more of the 2nd Royal Sussex. In the Sussex papers that I have seen now for a long time it seems that there is only one Battalion of the Royal Sussex Regiment fighting for the Country. I know the good old 4th Royal Sussex has done some good work. But they should not forget that after nearly fourteen months of fighting and huge sacrifices the old 2nd Sussex is doing a strong part in ridden Europe of a most dangerous and powerful enemy.

You asked me if there were any birds near the trenches. There are not many but in the summer I have spent many hours listening to the beautiful singing of the skylark. They even use to settle on 'No Mans Ground' as we call the spare ground between us and the Germans and no doubt built their nests there.

As I am writing this letter our guns are sending hundreds of shells over and destroying the German fortifications. It gives us courage to listen and know how freely our shells can be used. I have been outside to have a look at a squadron of our warplanes that are passing over, about twenty of them, all the same design and most probably going on a bombing expedition. It would make you all feel very uncomfortable to see about twenty German aeroplanes hovering over Arundel carrying as many bombs as they could, wouldn't it?

It is not such a good look out for me this year as it was last year this time, but we will look forward to a better year next year'.

MORRIS, ME - PRIVATE
ROYAL SUSSEX REGIMENT
REPORTED MISSING 1916

MORRISON, ALBERT PERCY - PRIVATE
2nd DORSET REGIMENT
King Street, Arundel

MORRISON, GEORGE EDWARD - PRIVATE
ROYAL ARMY SERVICE CORPS
King Street, Arundel

MOSELEY, JOSEPH - PRIVATE
ROYAL ENGINEERS
River Road, Arundel

MOSTYN, EHJ - CAPTAIN
ROYAL SUSSEX REGIMENT
Tower House, Arundel
WOUNDED IN AUGUST 1917

MOSTYN, EDWARD JEH - LIEUTENANT COLONEL
4th ROYAL SUSSEX REGIMENT
Tower House, Arundel
Ex Commanding Officer of the Arundel Territorial's,
DIED AT HOME JULY 1916

MOSTYN, JEH LIEUTENANT
4th ROYAL SUSSEX REGIMENT
Tower House, Arundel
Wounded in 1917

MOSTYN, JCM - CAPTAIN MC
ROYAL FIELD ARTILLERY
Tower House, Arundel
Awarded the Military Cross in 1917. Captain 'Cecil' who is the second son of the late Colonel Mostyn is a very popular young Officer and his many friends in Arundel will be gratified at the honour conferred on him.

MOSTYN, JOSEPH PD - SECOND LIEUTENANT
4th ROYAL SUSSEX REGIMENT
Tower House, Arundel
Just two weeks after the death of his father, Second Lieutenant Joseph Mostyn was wounded July 1916. Born in 1894 he was the great grandson of Sir Edward Mostyn, seventh Baronet. He enlisted at the beginning of the war and was commissioned in 1915. He was the third son of the late Lieutenant Colonel of the same Regiment

MYERSCOUGH, ROBERT - PRIVATE
4th ROYAL SUSSEX REGIMENT

MYERSCOUGH, WILLIAM - PRIVATE
4th ROYAL SUSSEX REGIMENT

NASH, A - STOKER
ROYAL NAVY
HMS BULWARK

NASH, ARTHUR - PRIVATE
DUKE OF CORNWALLS LIGHT INFANTRY
River Road, Arundel

NASH, GEORGE STANLEY - PRIVATE
11th ROYAL SUSSEX REGIMENT
River Road, Arundel
KILLED IN ACTION 1918

NASH, T - PRIVATE
QUEENS OWN ROYAL WEST SURREY REGIMENT
River Road, Arundel

NASH, W - ACTING SERGEANT
4th ROYAL SUSSEX REGIMENT
River Road, Arundel
WOUNDED 1916

A case of two brothers, Arundel lads, meeting at the Front after a long separation is recorded in a letter received by Mrs Nash of River Road from her son William. The elder brother Thomas joined the army and was last seen by his younger brother when he was 13 years of age and at school. Thomas who was in the Queens West Surrey Regiment was abroad at Gibraltar, Bermuda and South Africa for nearly six years and when he came home on a short leave before proceeding to France his younger brother had left to join the 2nd Battalion, the Royal Sussex Regiment and was at Dover, so they did not meet at home. The unexpected reunion on the battlefield gave both boys much delight and took place in April 1917.

NETLEY, W C - SEAMAN
ROYAL NAVY
HMS DRAKE

NEVILLE, WILLIAM EWART - SECOND LIEUTENANT
SUSSEX YEOMANRY
'A clerk in the Littlehampton Urban District Council's Offices before the war, he was a member of the Bognor Troop of Yeomanry and proceeded to the Dardenelles and afterwards Egypt. Second Lieutenant Neville, who is just over twenty five years of age, has many friends in this district, who will be glad to learn that he has so creditably won promotion'.
Gazetted Second Lieutenant in January 1918

NEWMAN, ARTHUR
10th ROYAL WEST KENT REGIMENT
South Marshes

NORTHEAST, FRANK - PRIVATE
Arundel
No Further Information other than he died
ROLL OF HONOUR

NORTHEAST, CHARLES GEORGE –SAPPER
ROYAL ENGINEERS
South Marshes, Arundel

NORTHEAST, JOHN BERNARD - PRIVATE
ROYAL SUSSEX REGIMENT
Arundel
DIED AT HOME 17 NOVEMBER 1916

Private John Northeast, was formerly employed at the Duke of Norfolk's stables and was a Territorial for nine years. Called up at the outbreak of war he trained at Salisbury Plain, then Newhaven, Horsham and Woolwich until seized by illness and discharged from the Army as medically unfit on March 24th 1916. Previous to the war he had enjoyed the best of health and never needed a Doctor. It is believed that his tuberculosis was originally induced by the lack of proper accommodation while at Newhaven. He and eleven comrades only had a barn to sleep in and they were flooded out of it. But for the kindness of a woman who accommodated them in her dwelling improvising beds as best she could they would have been without shelter. At Horsham his condition worsened by an attack of measles and exposure through the difficulty of finding him a separate billet. It was only after being taken from house to house that a room was found for him in which was another man also suffering with measles. Later under hospital treatment at Woolwich he seemed to have recovered and appeared to be well again, but at Chichester he was medically examined and discharged from the Army.
Returning home he had a relapse and gradually became weaker and passed away on November 17th leaving his wife and two children in severe financial difficulties.

NORTHEAST, JW - PRIVATE
KINGS OWN REGIMENT

NORTHEAST, MATTHEW - LANCE CORPORAL
4th ROYAL SUSSEX REGIMENT

NORTHEAST, WB - PRIVATE
4th ROYAL SUSSEX REGIMENT

NORTHEAST, WILLIAM JOHN SNR - PRIVATE
4th ROYAL SUSSEX REGIMENT

NORTHEAST, WILLIAM JOHN JNR - PRIVATE
ROYAL FIELD ARTILLERY

OLIVER, SIDNEY W - PRIVATE
1/1st BATTALION, THE LONDON REGIMENT, ROYAL FUSILIERS

O'NEILL, HJ - LANCE CORPORAL
MIDDLESEX REGIMENT

OSBOURNE, DB - LIEUTENANT
9th ROYAL SUSSEX REGIMENT &
ROYAL WEST SURREY REGIMENT
Arundel

The second son of Alderman Osbourne, Lieutenant Osbourne enlisted into the Royal Sussex Regiment in April 1915. In August 1917 he had attained the rank of Sergeant and was gazetted into the Royal West Surrey Regiment. Lieutenant Osbourne who was engaged at Brighton at the time he joined the Colours was a member of the Arundel senior football team some years ago. He had served in France for some sixteen months when he returned to England to prepare for his commission which he received in August 1917.

OSBORNE, WALTER MANSFIELD - CORPORAL
ARMY SERVICE CORPS
53 King Street, Arundel

OWENS, ALFRED - PRIVATE
ROYAL ARMY MEDICAL CORPS
Rock Cottage, Maltravers Street, Arundel

OWENS, F - PRIVATE
4th ROYAL SUSSEX REGIMENT

OXBORROW, ESW - MUSICIAN
ROYAL NAVY
HMS ALBEMARLE

PAGE, AJ - TROOPER
CITY OF LONDON YEOMANRY

PAGE, ALBERT THOMAS - PRIVATE
9th ROYAL FUSILIERS
KILLED IN ACTION 1918

PAGE, ERNEST - PRIVATE
16th ROYAL SUSSEX REGIMENT
KILLED IN ACTION 1918

PAPWORTH, WH - PRIVATE
EAST SURREY REGIMENT

PARKER, ARTHUR ERNEST - PRIVATE
1st BATTALION THE ROYAL SUSSEX REGIMENT
Tarrant Street, Arundel

PARKER, CHARLES ROYAL MARINE LIGHT INFANTRY
HMS HINDUSTAN

PARKER, GEORGE SERGEANT
ROYAL FIELD ARTILLERY

PARKER, WALTER - TROOPER
ROYAL FIELD ARTILLERY

PARSONS, AG - PRIVATE
4th ROYAL SUSSEX REGIMENT

PARSONS, AH - PRIVATE
ROYAL SUSSEX REGIMENT

PARSONS, EJ - SEAMAN
HMS ACTAECON ROYAL NAVY

PAVITT, ERNEST ALFRED – LANCE CORPORAL
5th BEDFORDSHIRE REGIMENT
4 Kirdford Road, Arundel

PATCHING, AH - PRIVATE
2nd ROYAL SUSSEX REGIMENT

PEARCE, RW - PRIVATE
3rd ROYAL SUSSEX REGIMENT

PEARSON, BERTRAM L - CAPTAIN MC & DSO
8 YORKSHIRE REGIMENT
Arundel
WOUNDED IN 1916

In November 1916, the then Lieutenant Bertram L Pearson of the 8th Yorkshire Regiment, the brother of Doctor Pearson, was awarded the Military Cross.
'For conspicuous gallantry and devotion to duty in leading his Company with great skill over difficult ground. He personally killed four of the enemy with his revolver and after being wounded for a second time, he lay in a shell hole giving all necessary orders until he fainted through loss of blood. He set a fine example of pluck and skilful leadership'
In October when a portion of an enemy trench had been captured he consolidated the position under heavy bombing and shell fire and it was to his organisation and example that three counter attacks were repulsed. The following evening when the captured trench was obliterated by heavy artillery he rallied his men, re-organised the position and inflicted further losses on the enemy.

PEARSON, CHARLES WE - PRIVATE
2nd ROYAL SUSSEX REGIMENT
WOUNDED ON 8 OCTOBER 1914

PEARSON, JBH - LANCE CORPORAL
2nd ROYAL SUSSEX REGIMENT
WOUNDED JULY 1916

PEARSON, RW - CAPTAIN/DOCTOR, MC
ROYAL ARMY MEDICAL CORPS ATTACHED TO
THE DURHAM LIGHT INFANTRY
Arundel
PRISONER OF WAR

Doctor Pearson was a well liked and respected man in Arundel where he practised. He volunteered to serve and endured a difficult time.

'There is much concern at the news that Dr. RW Pearson is reported wounded and missing on 27 May and everyone will share Mrs Pearson's consoling hope, for which a letter from a friend gives support that he is a prisoner of war. Dr. Pearson has been attached to the 22nd Durham Light Infantry for some months on the Aisne. His brother, in the Middlesex Regiment, was also reported missing on 27 May'.

Confirmation was soon received that Captain Pearson was a prisoner of war having been wounded twice himself and at the same time as details were released regarding the action in which he was awarded the Military Cross;

'For conspicuous gallantry and devotion to duty in the performance of his duties during lengthy operations. On one occasion two direct hits were obtained on his post and a patient who was being dressed was killed. On another day he followed the Battalion in a counter attack and rendered the most magnificent services to the wounded under heavy machine gun fire.

By his courage, fine example and great devotion he has at all times inspired his stretcher bearers and it was mainly due to him that so many of the wounded were got away by the bearers'.

Repatriated at the end of the war, 'news which was joyously received throughout the district, Dr and Mrs Pearson have gone to London for a few days'.

It was here that he received his Military Cross, presented by the King at Buckingham Palace, in the presence of Mrs Pearson.

PEARSON, WILFRED ARTHUR JOSEPH - PRIVATE
4th ROYAL SUSSEX REGIMENT
Bond Street, Arundel
Brother of Private CWE Pearson and Lance Corporal JBH Pearson

PECKHAM, HARRY - GUNNER
ROYAL FIELD ARTILLERY
Arundel
KILLED IN ACTION 1917

PEEL, FC - SECOND LIEUTENANT MC
4th ROYAL SUSSEX REGIMENT

Second Lieutenant Peel had been in the 4th Battalion the Royal Sussex since the outbreak of war. Having survived the landings and operations in Gallipolli he subsequently served in Egypt, holding the rank of Sergeant at the time. In July 1916 whilst attending a school of military instruction an accident occurred resulting in a bomb explosion in which the Captain of the Bombing Class lost his life and many men including Sergeant Peel were severely wounded. Some of the Officers attending the same class were so impressed by Sergeant Peel's actions following the accident they sent him a gift whilst he was recovering 'which will enable you to procure comforts while in hospital' and further wrote;
'We are sending you this as a mark of our esteem to you and also the devotion you showed at the time of the accident in that although wounded yourself you thought more of the welfare of the other men first and by your coolness and tact avoided a panic or even the slightest semblance of confusion'.
The West Sussex Gazette commented;
'Arundel people ill congratulate Superintendant Peel (his father) on his plucky sons escape and will wish him a speedy recovery'.
Sergeant Peel was commissioned Second-Lieutenant early in 1917
'As readers know, the popular young soldier has been serving with the 4th Royal Sussex since the outbreak of war; he took part in the landing at Gallipoli and subsequently served in Egypt, where at the school of military instruction, it will be remembered, he was wounded as the result of a bomb explosion by which the Captain of the bombing party lost his life'.
Ten months later Sergeant Peel was gazetted Second Lieutenant.
In June 1918 he came home on leave;
'Many friends have welcomed home on leave Lieutenant SC Peel, MC., Light Trench mortar Battery., 16th Royal Sussex Regiment, the only son of Police Superintendant Peel and Mrs Peel. He went out to the Dardenelles

with the 4th Royal Sussex Regiment and took part in the fighting at Sulva Bay. Later in Palestine he won the honour of the Military Cross. He was at the capture of Jerusalem and has seen over three years active service. His father, it is interesting to note, was formerly seven years in the Army and has now been in the Police Force for nearly twenty six years.

PERRY, JOHN THOMAS - SAPPER
ROYAL ENGINEERS
45 King Street, Arundel

PERRY, GEORGE PHILIP –PRIVATE
ARMY VETERINARY SERVICE
139 Park Bottom, Arundel

PEPPERALL, A - TROOPER
SURREY YEOMANRY

PESCOTT, ARTHUR - DRIVER
ROYAL ENGINEERS
South Marshes, Arundel

PESCOTT, EDWARD - PRIVATE
ESSEX REGIMENT
River Road, Arundel

PESCOTT, HENRY CHARLES - PRIVATE
2nd BATTALION THE ROYAL SUSSEX REGIMENT
Tarrant Street, Arundel

PESCOTT, GEORGE ERNEST - PRIVATE
ESSEX REGIMENT
River Road, Arundel

PESKETT, A
DETAILS NOT KNOWN

PETERS, JE - GUARDSMAN
GRENADIER GUARDS
An ex Arundel policeman
PRISONER OF WAR 1915

PETERS, WILLIAM HENRY
NO 1 DISPERSAL UNIT, DOVER
2 Verona Terrace, Arundel

PHILLIPS, D - PRIVATE
3rd ROYAL SUSSEX REGIMENT
Arundel

PHILLIPS, H - PRIVATE
4th ROYAL SUSSEX REGIMENT

PHILLIPS, HR - QUARTERMASTER SERGEANT
ROYAL ENGINEERS
Arundel Post Office Staff

PHILLIPS, JL - CO-QUARTERMASTER SERGEANT
7th EAST KENT REGIMENT

PHILLIPS, R - SAPPER
ROYAL ENGINEERS

PIERCE, THOMAS GEORGE - PRIVATE

ROYAL ARMY MEDICAL CORPS
Maltravers Street, Arundel

PILCHER, SJ - STOKER
ROYAL NAVY
HMS IRON DUKE

PITT, CAPTAIN
NATIONAL RESERVE

On duty with the Arundel detachment guarding the London to Dover
railway line in 1914

POAT, E - PRIVATE
9th ROYAL SUSSEX REGIMENT

POAT, J - PRIVATE
4th ROYAL SUSSEX REGIMENT

POAT, PR - SERGEANT
11th ROYAL FUSILIERS
WOUNDED IN APRIL 1917
EVACUATED TO THE GRAYLINGWELL WAR HOSPITAL,
CHICHESTER

POAT, WAV - SEAMAN
ROYAL NAVY
HMS AGINCOURT

POCOCK, F 1916
ROLL OF HONOUR

POTTER, CF - MAJOR
ROYAL FIELD ARTILLERY
Arundel
In June 1915 Major Potter was among the Officers whose names were
recommended for Distinguished Service in the Field in a despatch from Sir
John French. His grandfather was the founder of the 'West Sussex
Gazette'.

PRANGLE, REGINALD - PRIVATE
1st ROYAL WEST SUSSEX REGIMENT
BELIEVED TO HAVE DIED IN 1917

PRICE, SJ - TROOPER
12th LANCERS
Wounded in 1917

PRICE, THOMAS –PRIVATE
BEDFORDSHIRE REGIMENT
6 Norfolk Terrace

PULFORD, FG - LIEUTENANT
9th ROYAL SUSSEX REGIMENT
Arundel
An Arundel dentist before enlisting
WOUNDED IN SEPTEMBER 1915

PUTTOCK, A - PRIVATE
4th ROYAL SUSSEX REGIMENT

PUTTOCK, AA - PRIVATE
4th ROYAL SUSSEX REGIMENT

PUTTOCK, CLAUDE - PRIVATE
4th ROYAL SUSSEX REGIMENT
23 Bond Street, Arundel
PRISONER OF WAR APRIL 1917

Mr and Mrs Alfred Puttock, of 23 Bond Street, Arundel, received news in May 1917 that their son Claude, who was serving in France, had been missing since 27 April. They then had to endure an agonising three month wait before the news reached them that Claude had been made a prisoner of war and was being held in Germany.

PUTTOCK, GC - PRIVATE
4th ROYAL SUSSEX REGIMENT

QUINTON, GEORGE
BELIEVED KILLED IN ACTION 1917

RAIKER, M - PRIVATE
WEST RIDING MOBILISED BATTALION NATIONAL RESERVE

RALPH, RAYMOND = AIRMAN
RAF

RAPLEY, CECIL THOMAS - SERGEANT
4th ROYAL SUSSEX REGIMENT
High Street, Arundel

RATCLIFFE 1917
DECEASED, NO DETAILS

RATLEY, LAWRENCE - TROOPER
1st HOUSEHOLD DIVISION
Arundel
DIED OF WOUNDS 1917

RAWLINGS, EA - SEAMAN
ROYAL NAVY
HMS QUEEN ELIZABETH
LOST AT SEA

RAWLING, CHARLES
NO FURTHER INFORMATION

RAWLINGS, F - PRIVATE
ROYAL SUSSEX REGIMENT
WOUNDED IN 1916

RAWLINGS, GP - SENIOR SERGEANT
3rd ROYAL SUSSEX REGIMENT

RAWLINGS, GP JNR - PRIVATE
3rd ROYAL SUSSEX REGIMENT

RAWLINGS, P - SAPPPER
ROYAL ENGINEERS
Arundel

READ, ARTHUR H
NO FURTHER INFORMATION

READ, CHARLES HENRY - PRIVATE
4th ROYAL SUSSEX REGIMENT
KILLED IN ACTION 1917

READ, RICHARD JAMES REGINALD
7th AUSTRALIAN INFANTRY
KILLED IN ACTION 1915

READ, WILLIAM HENRY - PRIVATE
ROYAL FIELD ARTILLERY
King Street, Arundel

REDMAN, FV - CORPORAL
ARMY VETERINARY CORPS
Arundel

REDMAN, WC
REGIMENT UNKNOWN

REED, PW - PRIVATE
4th ROYAL SUSSEX REGIMENT

REED, RJ - PRIVATE
4th ROYALSUSSEX REGIMENT

REEVES, WILLIAM - PRIVATE
4th ROYAL SUSSEX REGIMENT

RICHARDSON, JF - PRIVATE
4th ROYAL SUSSEX REGIMENT

RICHARDSON, WILLIAM - PRIVATE
8th BUFFS
2 Wood View, Arundel

RISHMAN, FREDERICK GEORGE - SAPPER
ROYAL ENGINEERS
5 Arun Cottages, Arundel

ROBERTS, A - PRIVATE
4th ROYAL SUSSEX REGIMENT

ROBINSON, FW - PRIVATE
4th ROYAL SUSSEX REGIMENT

ROBINSON, GEORGE - PRIVATE
ROYAL ARMY SERVICE CORPS
DIED AT HOME 1918

ROBINSON, J - SERGEANT
ROYAL SUSSEX REGIMENT
WOUNDED IN 1918

ROBINSON, T - SERGEANT
ROYAL SUSSEX REGIMENT
WOUNDED IN 1917

ROGERS, CHARLES HENRY - PRIVATE
MACHINE GUN CORPS
KILLED IN ACTION 1917

ROGERS, HENRY GEORGE –PRIVATE
EAST SURREY REGIMENT
4 Kirdford Road, Arundel

ROGERS, JESSE CHARLES - CORPORAL
4th ROYAL SUSSEX REGIMENT
11 Wood View, Arundel
The 4th Battalion, the Royal Sussex Regiment were serving in Gallipolli in late 1915, from where Private JC Rogers, contracted a severe bout of dysentery. He was evacuated to Alexandria, Egypt and having been discharged on recovery was attached to the Headquarters Staff based there

ROGERS, THOMAS - CORPORAL
4th ROYAL SUSSEX REGIMENT
High Street, Arundel
A popular member of the 4th Royal Sussex Band, in which he played the cornet, Corporal Tommy Rogers enlisted into the Royal Hussars at the outbreak of war and served with them in France. He was awarded the Military Medal, for Conspicuous Gallantry during the fighting of the night of 10 and 11 April 1915.
Tommy was the son in law of Mr and Mrs Henson, who ran the tea rooms in Mill Lane, Arundel.

ROGERS, W - PRIVATE
3rd ROYAL SUSSEX REGIMENT

ROLLS, ALFRED J - GUNNER
ROYAL FIELD ARTILLERY

ROWE, GEORGE FREDERICK - PRIVATE
KINGS LIVERPOOL REGIMENT
South Marshes, Arundel

ROWE, PERCY FRANK - LANCE CORPORAL
2nd ROYAL SUSSEX REGIMENT
Causeway Villas, Arundel
KILLED IN ACTION 1915

RUMSEY, ARTHUR - SEAMAN
HMS MINITOUR

RUMSEY, AE - TROOPER
SUSSEX YEOMANRY
In December 1915 writing home from Gallipolli former West Sussex
Gazette Staff member writes;

'I am now attached to a bombing squadron, but it is not very comfortable
work when one gets one of John Turks thrown amongst us. Last night we
had our first baptism of Turkish rain. It rained for about half an hour and in
that time and I should say we had about six inches of it and we got
absolutely washed out of our dugouts. These are about one foot deep and
being perched on a hillside you can guess it run down pretty tidy. Down in
the main gully where all the water eventually reaches is mud up to the
wheel axles and in places they are stuck fast. We have had a new
experience lately having had to go down in the mines for six hours shifts
carrying out the dirt in sandbags. It's just as safe as being on top unless
John Turk manages to explode his first, if so one gets a rise in this world.'
In September 1918 he was given a new job;
'We are pleased to be able to state that Corporal AE Rumsey, late of the
Sussex Yeomanry, is now Corporal in charge of the Jerusalem Water
Works, the largest and most important in Palestine'.

RUMSEY, EDWARD - STOKER
ROYAL NAVY
HMS HERCULES and HMS DIDO
125 South Marshes, Arundel

RUMSEY, FF - PRIVATE
4th ROYAL SUSSEX REGIMENT
WOUNDED IN 1917

RUMSEY, GEORGE - LANCE CORPORAL
4th ROYAL SUSSEX REGIMENT
WOUNDED IN 1917

SADLER, WILLIAM JAMES - PRIVATE
ROYAL ARMY MEDICAL CORPS BOMBAY
14 Queen Street, Arundel

SALLOWS, J - GUNNER
ROYAL HORSE ARTILLERY

SAMPSON, CHARLES - PRIVATE
LABOUR BATTALION
31 Mount Pleasant, Arundel

SCOTT, WILFRED MM - GUNNER
ROYAL GARRISON ARTILLERY
KILLED IN ACTION 1917

SCUTT, AJ - PRIVATE
4th ROYAL SUSSEX REGIMENT

SCUTT, CJ - PRIVATE
4th ROYAL SUSSEX REGIMENT

SCUTT, E - PRIVATE
4th ROYAL SUSSEX REGIMENT
Wounded 1916

SCUTT, GEORGE - PRIVATE
4th ROYAL SUSSEX REGIMENT
DIED AT HOME 1915

SCUTT, HERBERT BRUCE - PRIVATE
ROYAL ARMY SERVICE CORPS
Orchard Place, Arundel

SCUTT WILFRED CHARLES MM
CANADIAN CONTINGENT
88 Surrey Street, Arundel
KILLED IN ACTION 15 SEPTEMBER 1916

SEAGRAVE, GT - PRIVATE
4TH ROYAL SUSSEX REGIMENT

SEARLE, WG - TROOPER
SUSSEX IMPERIALYEOMANRY

SHEPHERD, GEORGE LEMON - SAPPER
ROYAL ENGINEERS
Surrey Street, Arundel

SHERMAN, WILLIAM THOMAS - CAPTAIN
KINGS ROYAL RIFLES
157 King Street, Arunde
Retired and re-enlisted

SILVERLOCK, FE - PRIVATE
ROYAL ARMY MEDICAL CORPS

SILVERLOCK, JOHN - PRIVATE
4th ROYAL SUSSEX REGIMENT
Gratwicke Terrace, South Marshes, Arundel
KILLED IN ACTION 1915

SIMMONS, ALAN HUGH – PRIVATE
3rd BEDFORDSHIRE REGIMENT
7 Wood View, Arundel
PRISONER OF WAR

SIMMONS, PERCY JOHN – CORPORAL
2nd QUEENS REGIMENT
7 Wood View, Arundel
PRISONER OF WAR

SLAUGHTER, CHARLES - SAPPER
ROYAL ENGINEERS
King Street, Arundel

SLAUGHTER, CHARLES THOMAS - PRIVATE
ROYAL SUSSEX REGIMENT
ROYAL DEFENCE CORPS
DIED AT HOME 1917

SLAUGHTER, FRANK JNR - PRIVATE
Labour Corps
White Hart Inn, Queen Street, Arundel

SLAUGHTER, FREDERICK - COMPANY QUARTER MASTER SERGEANT
4th ROYAL SUSSEX REGIMENT
Abercrombie Inn, Queen Street, Arundel
'During the period February 25th to September 16th 1918 he has carried out his duties with the greatest energy and zeal. During operations near Grand Rozoy and in the line he has superintended the distribution of rations to his Company often under heavy fire, setting a fine example of devotion to duty. On one occasion near Kemmel in September the driver of the limber on which he was taking up rations was wounded by a shell. Though unaccustomed to animals he mounted and drove the limber himself bringing the rations to his Company'.

SLAUGHTER, T - PRIVATE
4th ROYAL SUSSEX REGIMENT
Arundel

SMART, FREDERICK ARTHUR OWEN - PRIVATE
4th ROYAL SUSSEX REGIMENT
Maltravers Street, Arundel

SMART, HARRY - PRIVATE
ROYAL ARMY SERVICE CORPS

The Royal Army Service Corps had a variety of jobs to perform, not the least in feeding the troops at the Front. Private Harry Smart was part of that organisation, based in 8th Field Bakery at a Supply Depot. In March 1915 he wrote to the West Sussex Gazette:
'Will you kindly allow me through your columns to the Mayoress of Arundel and others who subscribed to the Arundel parcel fund for soldiers

and sailors on active service. I am sure they appreciate what they have done for me and my comrades who are with the Expeditionary Force. I myself as a baker have not been in the firing line but have plenty to do to keep the supplies of bread up. Some of the soldiers who come down for a rest say what a good time we must have in the base. That is what they think. I might say we have not been up to our knees in mud but we've had it over the top of our boots and the conditions have been very bad all the winter. Our sleeping accommodation has only been tents and our beds the carpenter puts down with hammer and nails. Still it is all good for our country. I see by your issue of 26 January there are 63 on active service from Arundel, which I think is very good. But I should like to see an increase on the list for I feel sure that there are still a few men who could come forward and do their country a turn. The sooner they come forward the sooner we shall see the end. So come along boys, let's have a go'.

SMITH, ARCHIBALD - PRIVATE
1ST ROYAL FUSILIERS

SMITH, ARTHUR ALBERT PHILIPS – SERGEANT
2nd BATTALION THE ROYAL FUSILIERS
Park Bottom, Arundel

SMITH, B T - PRIVATE
ROYAL ARMY SERVICE CORPS
Hospital Attendant

SMITH, BERNARD THOMAS - SERGEANT
ARMY SERVICE CORPS
St Mary's Gate, London Road, Arundel

SMITH, C - LANCE CORPORAL
4th ROYAL SUSSEX REGIMENT

SMITH, E - PRIVATE
4th ROYAL SUSSEX REGIMENT

SMITH, F - PRIVATE
ROYAL ARMY MEDICAL CORPS

SMITH, GE - PRIVATE
9th ROYAL SUSSEX

SMITH, MICHAEL - PRIVATE
7th LONDON REGIMENT
Castle Stables, London Road, Arundel
KILLED IN ACTION 1918

SMITH, RT - PRIVATE
ROYAL ARMY SERVICE CORPS

SMITH, W - PRIVATE
4th ROYAL SUSSEX REGIMENT

SNOOK, B - PRIVATE
4th ROYAL SUSSEX REGIMENT

SPENCER, T - LIFEGUARD
2nd LIFEGUARDS

SPENCER, TF - PRIVATE
SOUTH LANCASHIRE REGIMENT
Wounded 1916

SPOONER, HARRY - PRIVATE
QUEENS ROYAL WEST SURREY REGIMENT
Kings Street, Arundel

STAMP, A J VICTOR - PRIVATE
4th ROYAL SUSSEX REGIMENT
Park Place, Arundel
KILLED IN ACTION 1917

STANDING, CHARLES – GUNNER
ROYAL GARRISON ARTILLERY
Arun Street, Arundel

STANDING, WILLIAM JAMES - ABLE SEAMAN
ROYAL FLEET RESERVE
HMS KING ORRY, ROYAL NAVY
Queen Street, Arundel

STANDING, WILLIAM JOHN – GUNNER
ROYAL GARRISON ARTILLERY
Arun Street, Arundel

STEDMAN, C - GUNNER
ROYAL FIELD ARTILLERY

STEDMAN, DAVID ERNEST - AIRMAN
ROYAL AIR FORCE
118 Queen Street, Arundel

STEDMAN, FRANK
118 Queen Street, Arundel

STEDMAN, GEORGE BERNARD - PRIVATE
9th EAST SURREY REGIMENT
River Road, Arundel
The second son of shoeing smith, Mr GF Stedman of River Road and Arun
Street, Cadet GF Smith enlisted with the Sussex Yeomanry. In May 1917
he was gazetted as a Second Lieutenant in the Royal Horse Artillery and
three months later was severely wounded in the face and shoulder and sent
to a Base Hospital in France where he made 'satisfactory progress'.
Before enlisting he was a member of the West Sussex Gazette Literary
Staff

STEDMAN, GF - TROOPER
SUSSEX YEOMANRY
Arundel

Commissioned in June 1917 into the Royal Horse and Royal Field
Artillery, formerly a West Sussex Gazette employee
Severely wounded in the face and shoulder on 7 September 1917 and in
hospital in France
WOUNDED IN 1917

STEDMAN, GB - PRIVATE
EAST SURREY REGIMENT
Wounded 1917

STEDMAN, JOSEPH EWART - PRIVATE
2nd MIDDLESEX REGIMENT
Arun Street, Arundel

STEVENS, AJD - PRIVATE
4th ROYAL SUSSEX REGIMENT

STEVENS, ERNEST - SECOND LIEUTENANT
7th DRAGOON GUARDS
Mount Pleasant, Arundel

Yet another Arundel soldier lad has been promoted from the ranks to 2nd
Lieutenancy in Sergeant Ernest Stevens. For sixteen years he has served
with the 7th Dragoon Guards and now receives his commission and
transference to the 2nd Shropshire Light Infantry. Lieutenant Stevens was
formerly a chorister in the Parish Church'.
Ernest Stevens was the son of Mrs Stevens of Mount Pleasant, Arundel and
had seen plenty of military service having fought all through the South
African War. When war broke out the 7th Dragoon's were based in India
and were sent to France as part of the Indian Cavalry Brigade, landing at
Marseilles in October 1914. He became an early casualty of the fighting in
December 1914, being wounded in the head and evacuated to the 1st
Eastern General Hospital, Cambridge.
He eventually returned to his Regiment and was in Alexandria in 1916,
when the news came that he was gazetted Second Lieutenant;
'For sixteen years Sergeant Stevens had served with the 7th Dragoon
Guards and has now received a commission and transference to the 2nd
Battalion the Shropshire Light Infantry. Sergeant Stevens was formerly a
chorister in the Parish Church choir and his father, who died many years
ago, was a member of the staff of the West Sussex Gazette'.

WOUNDED IN DECEMBER 1914

STEVENS, FREDERICK THOMAS - AIRMAN
ROYAL AIR FORCE
2 Co-operative Cottages, Arundel

STEVENS, GORDON HARRY - ACTING COMPANY QUARTER MASTER SERGEANT
BEDFORDSHIRE REGIMENT
2 Co-operative Cottages, Arundel

STEWART, WG - PRIVATE
4th ROYAL SUSSEX REGIMENT

STICKELLS, J - PRIVATE
4th ROYAL SUSSEX REGIMENT

STICKNEY, FRANK
4th ROYAL SUSSEX REGIMENT
'A well known young soldier, having been in the Duke of Norfolk's Estate Office for some years previous to the war, has been very seriously wounded in France. He has seen a lot of active service in the war and twice been in hospital with wounds and trench feet. So severe was his present injury that his brother was telegraphed for to go to France. Fortunately, it has been possible to bring the wounded lad to England and he is now in hospital in Aldershot'.

STILLWELL, G - CORPORAL
14th HUSSARS

STILLWELL, THOMAS RAWLINGS - LEADING SEAMAN
HMS BARHAM ROYAL NAVY
Surrey Street, Arundel,

STONE, ALFRED T – SECOND LEIUTENANT
4th ROYAL SUSSEX REGIMENT

The son of a long serving Royal Sussex soldier, whose family had lived in Arundel for some generations, Sergeant Stone was gazetted into the Royal Hussars in March 1915 with the rank of Second Lieutenant.

STONE, EP
ROLL OF HONOUR

STONE, FH - PRIVATE
4th ROYAL SUSSEX REGIMENT

STONE, FR - PRIVATE
4th ROYAL SUSSEX REGIMENT
Wounded July 1916

STONELY, GEORGE - PRIVATE
LABOUR CORPS CHICHESTER BATTALION
Tarrant Street, Arundel

STURT, ALFRED - SECOND LIEUTENANT
20th HUSSARS
Commissioned January 1915
'A Commission has been given to Sergeant Alfred Sturt, of the 20th Hussars, having received a Second Lieutenancy in that Regiment, in which he has a brother serving. He comes from an old Arundel family, his father, born and bred in the town saw long service in his son's Regiment and is now engaged in the remount business for the Government in Canada'.

STURT, EDWARD - OFFICERS STEWARD
HMS EUROPA ROYAL NAVY
Tarrant Street, Arundel

STURT, FREDERICK JAMES - SERGEANT
2nd ROYAL SUSSEX REGIMENT
Tarrant Street, Arundel
DIED OF WOUNDS 1916

STURT, HARRY - LANCE CORPORAL
7th ROYAL SUSSEX REGIMENT
Forming part of the New Army, the 7th Royal Sussex were moved to France in the spring of 1915. Lance Corporal Sturt, who many would have remembered as a good footballer in the Arundel team wrote home; 'We are having an exciting time and have only lost two of our Company to date. I am in good health'.

STURT, LESLIE - PRIVATE
ARMY SERVICE CORPS
7 Mountain View, Arundel

STURT, THOMAS – LANCE CORPROAL
1st ROYAL SUSSEX REGIMENT
Tarrant Street, Arundel
Serving in India

STURT, VICTOR - DRIVER
ROYAL FIELD ARTILLERY
Tarrant Street, Arundel

SUTER, ALBERT BYRON –AIRMAN
ROYAL AIR FORCE
13 Kirdford Road, Arundel

SWAN, ME - SQUAD SERGEANT MAJOR
SURREY YEOMANRY

SWAIN, FREDERICK - PRIVATE
3rd LONDON REGIMENT
KILLED IN ACTION 1917

SWAIN, GEORGE - PRIVATE
4th ROYAL SUSSEX REGIMENT
11 Gratwicke Terrace, South Marshes, Arundel
KILLED IN ACTION 1918

STYLES, JOSEPH - PRIVATE
8th EAST KENT REGIMENT
22 Kirdford Road, Arundel
KILLED IN ACTION 1915

TATE, W - PRIVATE
3rd ROYAL SUSSEX REGIMENT

TAYLOR, AG - PRIVATE
4th ROYAL SUSSEX REGIMENT

TAYLOR, AJ - LANCE CORPORAL
4th ROYAL SUSSEX REGIMENT

TAYLOR, BRUNO HENRY EDWARD - SIGNALLER
ROYAL NAVY
HMS BOMBALA
KILLED IN ACTION 1918

TAYLOR, HENRY VINCENT WALMSLEY - PRIVATE
LONDON REGIMENT
16 Bond Street, Arundel

TAYLOR, PHIL - FIRST CLASS PETTY OFFICER
ROYAL NAVY, HMS NELSON & HMS REINDEER

Serving on board a minesweeper, First Class Petty Officer Phil Taylor wrote in August 1915, clearly thinking of home:
'We have had terrible weather lately and could do with a few of Penfolds steam rollers round our way just to level things off a bit. Even in the midst of battle one pauses to consider how Slindons beans are progressing and Graffhams peas are sprouting. It is of such things of National importance that stir our Navy and makes them fight as they do (excuse the blot, the ship is rolling). I should like to thank all the people of Arundel who were responsible for sending me the beautiful parcel which I safely received'.
In January 1917 he was invalided back to Arundel for fifteen days leave, after an absence of two years and nine months:

'Among recent visitors on leave is Petty Officer Philip Taylor, a pensioner, who left the Castle at war's outbreak to re-join the Navy and found himself on board HM Minesweeper Reindeer. Taylor, who has been invalided home for fifteen days leave, after an absence of two years and nine months, has seen a lot of service in the Eastern Mediterranean. He has seen Turks and Germans galore and was close to the Clyde in the historic Gallipoli landing and could if he wished, tell many a great tale of Regiments and ships. His opinion of the Germans he has met and seen is very much to the point:

"They look just what they are, square headed beasts and criminals. If I was a Magistrate and any of them I have seen came before me, I would give them six months hard right off, without hearing what they had done. They can't help it, perhaps, that is just what they are".

TAYLOR, TIMOTHY WILFRED HAROLD - CORPORAL
ARMY SERVICE CORPS
16 Bond Street, Arundel

TESTER, ARCHIBALD EDMUND - LANCE CORPORAL, MM
4th ROYAL SUSSEX REGIMENT
River Road, Arundel
In June 1916 Lance Corporal Tester, a well known Arundel lad, who was actively associated with the local football team was awarded the Military Medal.
DIED OF WOUNDS 1917

TESTER, HE - PRIVATE
4th ROYAL SUSSEX REGIMENT
River Road, Arundel

THORN, G - PRIVATE
3rd HAMPSHIRE REGIMENT
1st WESSEX ROYAL FIELD ARTILLERY

TILL, FRANCIS - PRIVATE
5th CONNAUGHT RANGERS
Arundel
Arundel's youngest recruit
When Francis till enlisted in May 1915 he became Arundel's youngest recruit and was serving as a bugler.

TILLY, HERBERT WILLIAM - PRIVATE
ARMY SERVICE CORPS
High Street, Arundel

TRANAH, EAF - TROOPER
SUSSEX YEOMANRY
Trooper Tranah was the son of the Arundel Station Master and worked at the West Sussex Gazette before enlisting.
WOUNDED IN DECEMBER 1915 & SEPTEMBER 1918

TREAGUS, BERTRAM PERCIVAL – GUARDSMAN
COLDSTREAM GUARDS
1 Kirdford Road, Arundel

TRIMM, JOSEPH FRANCIS - GUNNER
ROYAL GARRISON ARTILLERY
Tarrant Street, Arundel

TRIGGS, J - GUNNER
ROYAL FIELD ARTILLERY

TULLEY, J - MUSICIAN
HMS EXMOUTH
River Road, Arundel

Writing to his parents, John Tulley, musician, serving on HMS Exmouth, says;
'I always get the West Sussex Gazette regularly every week, so I know pretty well all the news from Arundel. If you should see any member of the staff you might thank them for me, as I think it is very good of them to send the paper every week and I look forward to it. I should like them to know I appreciate their kindnesses'.

TULLEY, W - PRIVATE
River Road, Arundel
Wounded in July 1918

TWINE, GEORGE BERNARD - PRIVATE
4th &16th ROYAL SUSSEX REGIMENT
Maltravers Street, Arundel
WOUNDED IN NOVEMBER 1917

TYRWHITT-DRAKE, THOMAS - LIEUTENANT, MC & BAR
OXFORD AND BUCKINGHAMSHIRE LIGHT INFANTRY
Tower House, London Road, Arundel
Awarded the Military Cross in January 1917 followed by the Bar in
October 1917; He was the first Officer of his Regiment to be awarded the
Bar.

UPPERTON, ALBERT HENRY – FARRIER
ARMY VETERINARY CORPS
8 Wood View, Arundel

VICK, SYDNEY EDWARD - PRIVATE
13th ROYAL SUSSEX REGIMENT
KILLED IN ACTION 1918

WAITE, BERTIE THOMAS - STAFF SERGEANT
ROYAL AIR FORCE
6 Verona Terrace, Arundel

WAREHAM, HERBERT SIDNEY - PRIVATE
13TH LONDON REGIMENT
Mount Pleasant, Arundel
KILLED IN ACTION 4 JULY 1916

WAREHAM, WJ - PRIVATE
4th ROYAL SUSSEX REGIMENT

WASHINGTON, CH PRIVATE
ROYAL ARMY ORDNANCE CORPS
Eagle Inn, Arundel

'The loss of both feet is the price which has been paid in this war by Private Washington of the Royal Army Ordnance Corps, who formerly lived at Arundel where his brother ran the Eagle Inn, Tarrant Street. Only nineteen years of age, he had one foot shot off at Gallipolli and the other had to be amputated upon his arrival in hospital'.

The camp in which Private Washington was serving was heavily shelled by the Turks whilst he was in bed. His tent received a direct hit. His Chaplain, writing from Malta where he was recovering wrote;

'He is bearing up magnificently, an especially great effort on his part as he is so young'.

WOUNDED IN AUGUST 1915

WASHINGTON, CH - PRIVATE
4th ROYAL SUSSEX REGIMENT

WAITE, BT - CYCLIST
8th ESSEX REGIMENT

WATTS, DA -TROOPER
SUSSEX YEOMANRY

WEALE, EDWARD LANCELOT
ACTING CAPTAIN & ADJUTANT MC
THE PUBLIC SCHOOLS BATTALION ROYAL FUSILIERS
High Street, Arundel

Captain Weale enlisted a month after the war began and took his commission in December 1916. He had been in France for fifteen months when he was awarded the Military Cross 'for Gallantry and Devotion to duty' in September 1917;

'He handled his Company with great skill in the attack, captured all his objectives and took nearly two hundred prisoners. He consolidated the position and during the two following days he set a splendid example to his men under heavy shell fire'.

The son of Mr Edward Weale, the manager of the Capital and Counties Bank in the High Street and his wife,

WEEDON, PL - PRIVATE
3rd ROYAL SUSSEX REGIMENT

WELLER, GEORGE FRANCIS - COMPANY SERGEANT MAJOR
4th ROYAL SUSSEX REGIMENT
KILLED IN ACTION 1917

WELLS, WILLIAM HENRY JNR - PRIVATE
KINGS OWN YORKSHIRE LIGHT INFANTRY
High Street, Arundel

WEST, ARTHUR - PRIVATE
4th ROYAL SUSSEX REGIMENT
KILLED IN ACTION 1917

WEST, CHARLES - SERGEANT
7th ROYAL SUSSEX REGIMENT

Charles West was reported wounded in the autumn of 1916 and again in 1917.. He recovered and was next reported below nearly a year later; 'For most conspicuous gallantry near Epeh on September 18th 1918 when the Battalion was held up and driven back by severe machine gun fire he on his own initiative collected five men and followed one of our tanks closely and rushed a machine gun post on the outskirts of the village killing the team of six men and capturing two machine guns. Owing to the heavy fire from other strong points in the village he was unable to rejoin his Company but held this post for eight hours until the village had been mopped up. He did fine work'.
WOUNDED IN 1916 & 1917

WHEATLAND, ARCHIBALD - SAPPER
ROYAL ENGINEERS
Maltravers Street, Arundel

WHEATLAND, G - PRIVATE
4th ROYAL SUSSEX REGIMENT

WHEATLAND, W - PRIVATE
ROYAL ARMY MEDICAL CORPS

WILCOX, FRANCIS ALOYSIUS – PRIVATE
QUEENS ROYAL WEST SURREY REGIMENT
London Road, Arundel

WILLIAMS, WILLIAM JOHN ALFRED WALTER- PRIVATE
ROYAL ARMY SERVICE CORPS
South Marshes, Arundel

WHITTAKER, ARTHUR GLENDOWER
REGIMENTAL QUARTER MASTER SERGEANT 1916
SUSSEX YEOMANRY
High Street, Arundel

Mr Whittaker was the Clerk to the West Sussex Insurance Commission and an ex member of the Sussex Yeomanry which he rejoined at the outbreak of war. His father was an Arundel Alderman. The Sussex Yeomanry were sent to Gallipolli where many of them, including Corporal Whittaker contracted dysentery. He was reported as being dangerously ill, in hospital in Alexandria. Some weeks later in November 1915 his father received a cablegram to say that his son was 'progressing favourably'. Just before Christmas he was reported as being 'out of danger'.
SERIOUS DYSENTERY OCTOBER 1915, DISCHARGED AND EMPLOYED AT HEADQUARTERS

WILCOCK, CJ - COMPANY SERGEANT MAJOR
4th ROYAL SUSSEX REGIMENT
Tarrant Street, Arundel

October 1917; Yet another Arundelian has gained distinction in France, news having just reached Mr FC Wilcox of Tarrant Street that his son Cyril has been awarded the Military Medal. He has further been promoted from the rank of Lance Corporal to that of Sergeant and at the time of writing is acting as a Company Sergeant Major. This gallant lad in his letter gives no details of his award but briefly alludes to it;
'You'll be pleased to know that I have been awarded the Military Medal. Of course I haven't got the medal yet but it has appeared in orders and I wear the ribbon. Its quite posh of course and I am sending a bit to you'.
Accompanying the letter is a strip of the medal ribbon.

WILCOCK, FJ - PRIVATE
4th ROYAL SUSSEX REGIMENT

WILCOX, FRANCIS ALOYSIUS - PRIVATE
QUEENS ROYAL WEST SURREY REGIMENT
London Road, Arundel

WILLS, JOSEPH - PRIVATE
ROYAL NORFOLK REGIMENT
DIED IN INDIA 1918

WILSON, RE - FIRST CLASS SEAMAN
HMS VINDICTIVE
Arundel Post Office Staff
Son of Arundel Recruiting Officer

WILSON, VICTOR - LEADING SIGNALLER
HMS SHARK AND HMS FORTUNE
LOST AT SEA 1916

WITHERS, F = PRIVATE
4th ROYAL SUSSEX REGIMENT
WOUNDED IN JUNE 1916

WITHERS, W - PRIVATE
4th ROYAL SUSSEX REGIMENT
WOUNDED IN JULY 1916

WOOD, ARCHIBALD - CYCLIST
6th SUSSEX (CYCLIST) BATTALION
17 Bond Street, Arundel
Under training June 1917

WOOD, EDWIN J - CAPTAIN
ROYAL FIELD ARTILLERY
17 Bond Street, Arundel

'Mr and Mrs Wood have received intimation that their eldest son, Edwin, who was a Sergeant in the Royal Field Artillery when he left for the Front was given a commission in December 1914 and raised to the rank of Second Lieutenant. Sergeant Wood had not been in France very long before he was promoted to Quarter-Master Sergeant and the news of his further advancement will be received with pride and gratification by his fellow townsmen'.

WOOD, FREDERICK JAMES - PRIVATE
9th ROYAL SUSSEX
17 Bond Street, Arundel
PRISONER OF WAR 1915

WOOD, GEORGE STEPHEN - PRIVATE
9th ROYAL SUSSEX REGIMENT
17 Bond Street, Arundel
WOUNDED IN 1917

WOOD, LEONARD DANIEL - PRIVATE
4th ROYAL SUSSEX REGIMENT
17 Bond Street, Arundel
KILLED IN ACTION 1917

WOODWARD, ARCHIBALD BERNARD
ROYAL FIELD ARTILLERY
London Road, Arundel

WOODWARD, B - PRIVATE
3rd EAST KENT REGIMENT

WOODWARD, F SNR - PRIVATE
3rd ROYAL SUSSEX REGIMENT

WOODWARD, F JNR - PRIVATE
3rd ROYAL SUSSEX REGIMENT

WOODWARD, FRANK STEPHEN - GUNNER
ROYAL GARRISON ARTILLERY
London Road, Arundel

WOODWARD, LEONARD VICTOR - PRIVATE
GORDON HIGHLANDERS
London Road, Arundel

Printed in Great Britain
by Amazon

15665000R00099